Eddie Spirer
The Little Minister

by Ross F. Hidy

Purple Pomegranate Edition
Printed in cooperation with the
Lutheran History Center of the West
and Jews for Jesus

Purple Pomegranate Productions
80 Page Street, San Francisco, CA 94102

A special edition published as a joint project of
The Lutheran History Center of the West, 5242 Park Highlands
Boulevard, Concord, CA 94521-3706
and Jews for Jesus,
60 Haight Street, San Francisco, CA 94102

Published by Purple Pomegranate Productions,
a division of Jews for Jesus

Cover design and illustration by Sue Saunders

96 97 98 99 00   9 8 7 6 5 4 3 2 1

Second edition
ISBN 1-881022-21-8

Edward Nathaniel Spirer, while attending
Western Seminary in Nebraska, 1929

Foreword

"Eddie Spirer was an original!" That's how pastor Christian Thearle described the man who encouraged him to become a minister. Pastor Thearle was just one of the thousands of people touched by Eddie Spirer.

I never knew his full story until I took down the oral history of the then 92-year-old retired Lutheran minister. After hearing Eddie's story, I understood how this Orthodox Jew became a Christian and later a pastor. Touched by the story, I decided that I had to write Eddie's biography.

When word got out about what I was doing, the letters started to come. Many people wanted to share their stories about how much Eddie had meant to them, how this little Jewish minister had touched their lives.

At Eddie's funeral, Bishop Lloyd Burke said, "Eddie came from the East, saw a star, brought a hammer, nails and a saw, and built churches all over the Southwest, all to glorify God!" This little converted Jew served his Lord for sixty-one years here on this earth. Many of us knew and loved "The Little Minister." After you read his story, I think you will, too!

Ross F. Hidy,
Concord, California

Eddie Spirer

The Little Minister

"If you won't give up this foolishness," Eddie's father glared, "then you'll have to get out!"

The inevitable blowup had finally come. "I'll leave in the morning," Eddie Spirer quietly conceded as he clutched the book his father had denounced. Eddie knew all such material was forbidden in his home. And he knew exactly why: the Spirers were Orthodox Jews. For that reason, it was not a surprise that his father became furious when he discovered a Bible in Eddie's room—a Christian Bible, complete with both covenants. The confrontation was a somber moment, a moment of truth. No further words passed between father and son. As Eddie began to pack his bags, he could hear his mother downstairs, sobbing. She had heard the entire exchange and she knew the choice her son had made. In the silence of his room, Eddie wiped away a few tears of his own, for he knew his life would never be the same.

Eddie slowly stuffed shirts, pants and socks into his bags on that last night in the house of his childhood—the house where he had shared seder meals with his two brothers and his sister, the house where his mother had lit shabbat candles and his father had recited the traditional prayers, the house he could no longer call home. He hand picked his keepsakes as he packed: two family photos, a favorite jacket and his Bible.

The next morning, Eddie withdrew his entire life savings from the bank and boarded a westbound train. The year was 1921. The destination was Los Angeles.

Why had such a likable and successful Jewish boy made such a drastic decision? Eddie Spirer had embraced Jesus Christ as his Messiah. To his Jewish family, this was anathema. To Eddie, it was the truth that fulfilled every need he had ever known. It was the good news that would set the course of his entire life.

Eddie (standing, fifth from the left) at a dinner party with his family in Wilmington, Delaware, c. 1905

The Long Ride Across America

Somewhere between his hometown of Wilmington, Delaware and Chicago, Eddie closed his eyes and allowed himself to ponder all he had left behind. He smiled as he remembered his bar mitzvah when he was twelve. He could almost taste his mother's wonderful meals—the blintzes, the latkes, the gefilte fish. He could almost hear the humming of saws and the pounding of hammers as his father taught him how to work with wood. Eddie had wanted to learn to be a carpenter so that he could help his father in his construction business. While in school, Eddie built an oak desk for a teacher and little presents for his mother. Later he studied architecture at the University of Pennsylvania, and eventually he helped his father renovate buildings.

One remodeling job stood out, not because the task was so unusual but because of someone Eddie met. When Eddie presented an estimate on the remodeling job to the owner of the Toplis store, he knew it might be high, so he offered to do the work on a "cost-plus" basis. Mr. Toplis agreed as long as he could pay the workers directly each week. Each Friday Eddie brought the payroll figures to Toplis's bookkeeper, Wilhelmena Dettling. Each week she prepared the checks, and each Friday she said to Eddie, "Please come and visit my church." She repeatedly extolled the wonders of Zion Lutheran. . . As the wheels clicked on the rails, Eddie chuckled. He remembered how long he had hesitated before visiting Mena's church. What if someone from the synagogue saw him? That would be tantamount to denying his family, at least in the eyes of his Jewish people.

Each Friday when Mena would ask Eddie to come to church, he began to soften. As each week passed he became more and more curious. Why would this gentile woman be so intent on Eddie considering Jesus as the Messiah?

Eddie, second from right, with his sister Mildred and brothers Irvin and Frank, enjoying Augustine Beach, Florida, 1920.

Eddie Goes to Church

Finally, one Sunday night Eddie mustered enough courage at least to

4

approach the church. He walked around the block a couple of times; then, taking a deep breath, he slowly went up the six steps to the front door. He walked into the narthex, but didn't hear a thing. Maybe they are praying, he thought. He peeked through the crack between the wooden doors to the sanctuary, but he could only see directly down the aisle. As he leaned against the doors, trying to hear something, anything, the doors creaked loudly and swung open. There he was, Eddie Spirer, an Orthodox Jew, in a Christian church!

Hoping he would not be noticed, he climbed the stairs at the side of the sanctuary and took a seat in the balcony.

The people seemed friendly enough. But the hymnal posed a problem. Every time Eddie came across the name "Jesus" or "Christ" he covered it with his thumb.

After the service, Mena introduced Eddie to the pastor who gave him a Christian Bible and a service book. Eddie accepted the gifts, for he had never read the New Testament. He knew, however, that at home he would have to hide them because such books were banned by his father.

Eddie Ready to Learn

Eager to learn about this Jesus of Nazareth, Eddie spent weeks studying. As Eddie read, he wondered if Jesus was the promised Messiah. This was quickly becoming the most important question of his life. The more he read, the more determined he became to find the truth.

The fact that the Christian Bible contained an Old Testament as well as a New Testament reassured Eddie. He could see that to believe in Jesus he did not have to give up all he had been taught and believed as a Jew.

By this time, Eddie wanted to know more about Jesus. He read and reread the Gospels. In the first chapter of Matthew, he found a clear reference to a prophecy of Isaiah. This promised the coming of a Messiah, Emmanuel, God With Us. Matthew refers to many Old Testament prophecies and shows how they were fulfilled by Jesus. This soon became Eddie's favorite gospel. He also enjoyed reading Mark because it is packed with action and stories about the power of Jesus. In Luke, he read of Jesus' tender mercies and in John the great mystery of the opening verses. It was not yet clear to him what all this meant, but he could not put down the book.

Eddie read John 1:17: "For the law was given by Moses, but grace and truth came by Jesus Christ." He knew that Moses had given the law. But the law had never given him any peace, just guilt feelings about his inability to match up. With this verse, Eddie saw another side of God—a God of compassion and mercy. In Jesus, Eddie was discovering a loving God, not the angry God he had always envisioned—not a God of judgment, but a God of forgiveness.

As much as Eddie poured over the Gospels, he couldn't take the big step. He kept visiting Zion Lutheran Church, but he couldn't make a commitment.

Eddie attended the University of Delaware and the University of Pennsylvania from 1913 to 1918.

Someone suggested that Eddie visit Messiah Lutheran Church in Philadelphia. The name "Messiah" piqued his interest, so he went. The big electric sign over the front door, "The Friendly Church," intrigued him, so he entered.

What an experience! The church was packed and Eddie had to go up to the balcony to find a seat. As he sat down, he saw the sign in front of the sanctuary that spelled out JESUS in large electric letters. There was no doubt about what these people believed! And the music was stunning. Eddie had never before heard eleven hundred people singing such joyful hymns.

After the service, Eddie met Ross Stover, the pastor. Eddie, standing only five-feet even, had to look up at Dr. Stover, who was six-foot-two, but his friendly and warm handshake made Eddie feel welcome. When Eddie said he was a Jew who was trying to decide if Jesus was the Messiah, Dr. Stover suggested he talk with Pastor Morentz, their missionary for the Jewish people.

Eddie Embraces the Promised Messiah

As Eddie left church that night, he knew that he had already decided. Jesus was indeed the promised Messiah, and Eddie wanted to follow him.

Eddie later met with Pastor Morentz. They studied the Bible together, and Eddie saw how perfectly Jesus fulfilled the prophecies of the Old Testament.

Eddie never told his parents about his decision to follow Jesus. But he thought perhaps his father knew, or at least feared it might happen. Perhaps his father sensed how much Eddie had changed. Why else would he have lost his temper and demanded that Eddie stop reading the New Testament or leave home?

Eddie's Damascus Road

Eddie opened his eyes as the train pulled into the station in Chicago. There he transferred to a train bound for Los Angeles, which was about as far away as he could get from Wilmington and still be in the United States. Every time the train stopped at a town, Eddie got out to stretch his legs taking his New Testament with him. As the train moved west, he read and reread about the life and teachings of Jesus. Reading through the Acts of the Apostles, Eddie related to Saul of Tarsus. He saw his train ride as his Damascus Road. Before the train reached California, Eddie was positive he had made the right decision. But when he actually arrived in Los Angeles, the magnitude of his choice hit him. Eddie later recalled:

> As I stood on the station platform, three thousand miles away from my loved ones, many thoughts raced through my mind. Was I really a traitor to my people and thus deserved this self-imposed banishment from hearth and home? Was I disobedient to the fourth commandment that enjoins us to honor our fathers and mothers? To my dying day I shall remember that parting scene from my mother. It was almost more than I could bear to hear the continuous sobbing of my mother and see the face stained with tears that had been flowing all the previous day. But hard as the ordeal was, my duty was clear. The still small voice of the Master bade me go on, and I could not be disobedient to the heavenly vision.

In Los Angeles, Eddie registered at the Baltimore Hotel, inexpensive but adequate. The first Sunday, he found his way to First Lutheran Church. "I am an Orthodox Jew," he told Pastor W. S. Dysinger, "but I want to be baptized, for I believe that Jesus was the Messiah." Convinced of Eddie's sincerity, Pastor Dysinger welcomed him into the new members' instruction class.

A few weeks later, Eddie publicly confessed his faith in Christ as Lord and Savior and was baptized. Now that he was a baptized member of the Lutheran Church, Eddie felt a new peace and joy. He had to tell Mena the news. That night he wrote her a letter. He smiled as he sealed the envelope, knowing that she would be very pleased.

Eddie the Carpenter

Finding work was tougher than finding a church. There were no openings for architects, and although there were jobs for carpenters, Eddie's tools were in Delaware. Soon his bank account was getting low. He would just have to trust God to take care of his needs.

Sure enough, the Harris Brothers Hardware Store offered Eddie credit on all the tools he wanted. The next day he

Dena Markowitz Spirer, Eddie's mother, 1940.

7

landed a carpenter's job helping a crew jack up a house to put an apartment under it. This was heavy work, harder than anything he had ever done. But God had answered and Eddie had a paycheck.

Eddie wrote his mother telling her about California, his job and his joining the Lutheran church. He knew this would upset his father, but resolved that they should know.

Working with heavy timbers, Eddie's hands soon became blistered and were raw. The foreman noticed and concluded that the work was too heavy for him. "Can you do finish work?" the foreman asked. When Eddie assured him that he could, he was sent to Beverly Hills to work on a fine house.

He worked in the servants' quarters in the back of the house, easy work putting picture molding around the top of the ceiling. He was so relieved to have this kind of work that he lost no time. He stepped up on the benches, "Bang, bang, bang," then climbed down and moved the bench. When another carpenter looked in and saw how fast Eddie was working, he said, "Hey, slow down. You can't do that. You do that and all of us will get canned!"

Slowing down made the job even easier, and Eddie enjoyed it. The pay was good, so each week he stopped by the hardware store and soon had the entire debt paid off. Eventually he landed a job as a construction foreman.

Eddie was a busy man. He worked steadily. He moved into his own apartment. He shopped and prepared his own meals. The church became his family. Every week he attended the Luther League; often joining the group for picnics or outings to the beach. And once a week Eddie wrote Mena a long letter. She always answered with news of his hometown.

Rejected Because of His Faith

One day, walking down the street, Eddie was surprised to hear someone call out his name. "Eddie! Eddie Spirer. I can't believe my eyes!" It was a

Eddie, right, with co-workers Frank Gorster and John Grim, labored as a carpenter in Southern California, 1924.

high school friend who was now in the navy. He almost shouted, "I heard that you were dead—your family had your funeral!"

Eddie was startled, but not shocked. He had wondered if that would happen after he wrote to his mother about his baptism. He told his old friend that Jewish families sometimes do that when a relative becomes a Christian. He had been hoping and praying that his father might have a change of heart. Now he knew that what he feared might happen had actually happened. It was official: his family ties were cut.

His father's actions hurt. Now, as never before, Eddie felt alone. He later wrote:

Isn't it sad? A Jew may be an atheist and he will still be considered a member of Israel, but let him believe in Christ and he is cursed and cut off from the nation. I knew God in Judaism, but I never loved Him. I learned to know Him in Christ, and He won and changed my heart. In accepting Christ I have not accepted another God who rivals Jehovah, but in Christ, God came to possess me and I Him. Whereas before I knew God as an It, a mighty power which I feared, now He is a person manifested in the loving and redeeming Christ, and dwells in my heart through the Holy Spirit. As a Jew I knew the law: "And this is the law which Moses set before the children of Israel" (Deut. 4:44). As a Christian I have discovered God's love, and now I know a new peace. "But grace and truth came by Jesus Christ" (John 1:17).

For Eddie's family, he was dead. In a strange way, this fortified Eddie's link to his Jewish heritage.

The Psalmist provided comfort. Eddie read and reread the verses that had consoled his people during the dark chapters of their lives: "Yea, though I walk through the valley of the shadow of death, I shall fear no evil, for thou art with me" (Psalm 23).

The Gospel of Matthew bolstered Eddie's resolve to keep the faith: "Blessed are those who are persecuted for righteousness' sake, for theirs is the kingdom of heaven." When anger against his father would well up, Eddie turned to another verse: "If you love those who love you, what reward have you?"

It was as if Jesus were speaking, just as he had spoken long ago. Eddie knew he had to love and forgive. Each day he prayed for his father and the rest of his family. And he came to trust in the words of the loving God found in the Gospel of Matthew, "Lo, I am with you always, to the end of the age" (28:20).

Eddie's First Convention

One year Eddie was elected as a delegate to the annual Convention of the

California Synod. It was held in San Bernardino. Eddie roomed with another delegate in a small vacant apartment. There was little furniture in the room except for the double bed that pulled down from the wall. When they arrived, Eddie and his roommate, a very large man, sat down on the bed and talked. After a while Eddie stretched out to rest and the other man left the room to clean up for dinner. When the man returned to the room, Eddie and the bed were gone! The Murphy bed had lifted back up pinning Eddie against the wall. His new friend pulled the bed back down to free Eddie, and they both roared with laughter.

Eddie wrote to Mena about the convention and all of his adventures. A few weeks later, he received a letter from her with bad news. His father had been badly injured in a construction accident. A freight elevator door had malfunctioned, remaining open after the elevator descended. Seeing the open door, Eddie's father stepped into what he thought was the elevator compartment. He fell and died from his injuries a few days later.

Eddie regretted that he and his father were never reconciled. After his father's death, however, he began to correspond with his mother and other family members.

A Cure for Homesickness

Eddie's friends at church were like a second family, but he was still homesick. Nothing in California could ease his deep yearning for his own family. Also, Eddie wanted his own home. He wondered what Mena would say if he asked her to marry him. The idea grew so strong that Eddie decided to try!

His letter was to the point: "Mena, will you marry me and come West and make a new home here with me in California?" As he dropped the letter in the mailbox, Eddie prayed that what he had done was right. He felt certain that God was leading him.

When Mena read the letter, she was shocked. She had grown to like Eddie, but marry him? That would mean the biggest change in her life. She had never left home. Moreover, she was nine years older than Eddie.

Mena had hoped that someday she would fall in love and marry, but she had never even had a boyfriend. For a week she prayed and thought about the proposal. Finally she wrote Eddie a letter. She told him that just thinking about riding alone on a train all the way across the country to California terrified her. There was no way she could go out West to marry Eddie.

Quick with a solution, Eddie promised to meet her in Chicago. That way Mena would only have to spend one night alone on the train. She felt she could manage that.

Mena was excited but she tried not to show it. She kept her wedding plans a secret because she was positive that her mother would never approve. It was hard to leave without her mother's blessing, but somehow she managed to get her things together and board a train bound for Chicago. When the train arrived, Eddie was waiting on the platform.

The wedding was quiet and small, held at a nearby Lutheran church. The newlyweds stayed one day in Chicago and then set out for Los Angeles. Needless to say, Mena's mother was stunned when she received a letter declaring that she now had a son-in-law.

Settling Down in L.A.

On the train ride to California, Mena was fascinated by the scenery. In Los Angeles, the newlyweds set up housekeeping in a small rented cottage. Their funds were low, but their hopes were high.

Mena found a secretarial job; Eddie continued his construction work. They joined Hollywood Lutheran Church, where they soon found warm friends.

The months sped by. On their first anniversary, Eddie wanted to buy Mena a special gift. But he was frustrated because he had no money. That day, to save his ten-cent trolley fare, he walked home from work. On the way, he went into a hardware store and explained that he needed a little something to give to his wife. The salesman found a free yardstick for him—this was the anniversary present. After dinner, Eddie and Mena took a walk. With the dime he had saved, he bought two ice cream cones. It wasn't much of a party, but they were happy—and they used the yardstick in their home for years.

At this time Los Angeles was experiencing a building boom, so carpenters had no trouble finding work. A fellow carpenter kept pestering Eddie, "We should go into business for ourselves and be contractors because that is where the money is!" Eddie hesitated, pointing out that he had no money to buy supplies to get started.

But his friend didn't give up on the idea. Soon he had made a key contact. He had met a man who wanted to build a court with six houses but had no working drawings. It was a perfect opportunity for an experienced architect such as Eddie! He worked as a carpenter during the day and prepared the plans at night. When he and his friend presented the design to the man, they got the job!

The two new contractors had enough cash to buy sand—that was cheap. At the lumber yard, they showed the receipt for the sand and were able to get the lumber on credit. Soon they were able to obtain all the materials, and their first construction project was under way.

Eddie Almost Dies

The first job was a success—the owner was very happy. This, of course, led to other jobs. Eddie and his partner's reputation grew, and so did their paychecks. Everything went smoothly. In fact, things were going so well that Eddie refused to worry when he began gaining weight and his body became bloated. After all, he was now happily married—many men put on weight when they settle down. Eddie was confident that he would be all right. But he was wrong.

The new pastor at Hollywood Lutheran Church, Dr. Milton Stine, was worried. He asked a physician to examine Eddie. When the test results came back, the news was not good. Eddie had acute nephritis. He had to enter the hospital immediately. How long would he be out of commission? Three days, three weeks, three years? The doctor didn't know. But he did say that the disease was serious and sometimes fatal. At that time there were no effective antibiotics.

Worried, Mena stayed at the hospital to care for Eddie as often as possible. Somehow they managed to get by on her meager salary earned as secretary.

In the hospital, one doctor after another examined Eddie. Each one went through the same process, pushing a finger in his chest and looking at the indentation that was left. For three years Eddie was in and out of the hospital. He was unable to work, so he had lots of time to read the Bible. He read the Psalms so many times he knew them by heart.

Many people visited Eddie. One he never forgot was a retired minister, "Daddy" Streeter. Streeter told Eddie, "Brother, I believe that if you will give yourself to God and work for Him, God will spare your life."

Eddie was not so sure. "What could I do for God?" he asked.

The wise minister responded with a question: "If God saw fit to spare your life you could tell others about Him, couldn't you?" Daddy Streeter left Eddie to ponder the thought.

Later that day a nurse, who had just looked over Eddie's charts, rushed into his room and told him that he was going to die! He knew he was sick, but the seriousness of it had not really hit him until after he heard her grim prediction.

Eddie's Commitment to Serve—If He Is Healed

Later he wrote about what went through his mind: "That night I settled it. I made a real commitment to the Lord and asked God to heal me. The next morning the doctor came in, sat on the edge of the bed, and began telling me how serious my condition had become. I said to him, 'Oh, forget it, Doctor!' Then I told him about the minister's visit and that last night I had made this commitment that I would serve the Lord if He would spare my life. The doctor looked at me and shook his head. But I was positive God had heard my prayer."

God not only heard the prayer, but He answered it. Eddie got better. He left the hospital and went home to Mena. Everyone who visited heard what God had done—at least for a while.

Habits are hard to break. "I went back to my old ways, looking for the almighty dollar," Eddie admitted. One day he responded to an ad for a building inspector position. This would be easy work, even for someone who had been so ill, he reasoned. And the pay was terrific. On his way to meet with the chief inspector, Eddie felt weak. Instead of meeting with the man who could hire him, he went home thinking that he might return the next day. He never did apply for that job.

Eddie and Mena moved into a new apartment, and for a while his health improved. Then a very good job offer came along. A woman who wanted to build a home in Venice (near Los Angeles) pleaded for him to do the plans. Aware of his health problems, she told Eddie to take his time. Because his funds were low, he took the well-paying job.

But his health suffered. One night he was so confused he didn't even know where he was. "I felt I was way up on the top of the bed and could not get down," he later described. "I was a mess."

A frantic Mena called the doctor. He came to see Eddie, but said he had done all he could and would have to leave it in the hands of the "greater physician." He gave Eddie a shot and left him to rest.

"I was able to hear the doctor distinctly," Eddie said. "And I cried out, 'Lord, I know I have been a disappointment to You, but if You give me another chance I will make good.'" Then Eddie fell asleep and slept soundly. It was about that time that Dr. Ross Stover came from Philadelphia to visit his mother, who was living in Hollywood. Dr. Stover had been a great influence on Eddie and was one of his heroes. Eddie's spirits lifted when Dr. Stover surprised him with a visit.

After talking with Eddie for a few minutes, the tall, smiling minister knelt by the bed and prayed that God would heal his little Jewish friend. "I felt like I was a changed man again," Eddie said. "I could see that all of those people had been coming in offering me jobs and I had backtracked." Years later Eddie pointed to Dr. Stover's visit as the turning point in his life.

Telling Others About the Messiah

After Eddie's health improved, he decided he had to start telling others about Jesus the Messiah. He felt a special concern to reach his own Jewish people. Bloated condition and all, Eddie enrolled in a nearby Baptist Bible school. He discovered that one class, practical theology, really was street preaching. He was to accompany a man assigned to Jewish ministry. They ventured to Brooklyn Heights area of Los Angeles, a Jewish neighborhood.

One day, when they could not gather a crowd on a street corner, the missionary asked Eddie to climb up onto a chair and preach in Yiddish. Eddie started with the story of Abraham, Sarah and Isaac. Jewish people stopped to listen, curious. "Isaac was their only son, but the Bible tells of another son," Eddie turned the corner in his sermon knowing he had his audience hooked. "The prophets had said that God would send His Son, the Messiah and Jesus

13

Eddie and his wife, Mena, in Nebraska, c. 1930.

was born in Bethlehem." As soon as he mentioned the name of Jesus, eggs and over-ripe tomatoes started flying. "I got plastered," Eddie later laughed. What a mess! The onslaught broke up the street meeting and the pair had to flee. As Eddie was running away, one Jewish person shouted, "We ought to crucify you!"

Did this discourage Eddie? No. It just buoyed his faith. He told Mena, "Now I know how Saul of Tarsus felt when he tried to tell the Jewish people about the Messiah. He didn't stop and neither will I."

Faith Tested on the Way to Seminary

A new pastor, Dr. J. George Dorn, arrived at Hollywood Lutheran and encouraged Eddie to enroll at the nearest Lutheran seminary. This meant going to Fremont, Nebraska! Western Seminary accepted Eddie as a special student for the fall semester the next year. At the seminary's request, he prepared himself with a study program under the tutelage of Dr. Dorn and another minister.

In late November, Eddie received a check for twenty-five dollars from a man in Hawaii. It was to go toward his seminary expenses. The next day, Eddie visited a friend who had just lost his job. Eddie asked if he could do anything to help. His friend's wife replied, "If I had twenty-five dollars, I could pay these bills." Eddie took out the money he had just received and gave it to her.

When Eddie got home, Mena wasn't exactly excited about her husband's generosity. "Why did you do that?" she said regretfully, "Why didn't you just give her ten dollars?"

"She asked for twenty-five dollars," Eddie shrugged, feeling he had done as he should. His opinion didn't change when, later that day, their landlord informed them that their water would no longer be included in their rent.

The next day, when Mena headed for the water office to see how much they should expect to pay, Eddie went to the post office. There was no mail for Spirer, but on a whim, he asked if there was anything for "Edward." Sure enough, Mena's sister had written to tell about a missionary meeting held in her home. The people had taken up an offering for mission work and decided to send it to Eddie. Enclosed with the letter was a check for twenty-five dollars!

This type of miraculous money management happened again and again as Eddie and Mena learned to trust God. Eddie often said, "The cattle of a thousand hills are His. God will provide."

Their faith was stretched in another way, too. In September 1929 they headed east to the seminary in Fremont, Nebraska. They prayed that the car would start each morning, and they prayed that it would keep going all day long. They arrived with just thirty-eight cents in their pockets.

Life in seminary was a potpourri of new experiences. The professors quickly realized that Eddie not only knew the Bible, but also knew Hebrew. In a way, that put him one step ahead of many students. Eddie and Mena moved into the dorm. On Sundays he helped supply vacant pulpits. For a while he preached at a Lutheran church in the town of Papillion. Eddie enjoyed his studies and his new friends, but not the shoveling of snow he thought he left behind in Delaware.

Home for the Holidays

Homesick, Eddie and Mena visited their families in Wilmington at Christmas (and Hanukkah). Mena had not seen her mother since she had eloped. They had a wonderful reunion with both families.

For Eddie, the trip brought back memories of his decision to become a Christian. The choice to be "a Jew for Jesus" had not been easy. When he visited Pastor Morentz at the office of the Lutheran Mission to the Jews, he was asked to write an article for the *Messiah Hebrew Quarterly*. In the article, "The Power of the Gospel," Eddie described his pilgrimage:

> My conversion dates back to the early days of the Philadelphia Mission to the Jews when I had the privilege to be brought in contact with Pastor

Western Seminary, Fremont, Nebraska.

15

Eddie preaches his senior sermon, 1930, at Western Seminary, Fremont, Nebraska

Morentz after hearing him preach in Zion Lutheran Church, Wilmington, Delaware. The old friends of the mission will remember part of the story, repeated here for the benefit of new friends of the cause of Christ among his ancient people. Facing after my conversion the usual hostility on the part of my orthodox Jewish parents and friends and realizing what it might mean to me materially and spiritually, situated in a comparatively small city, I decided to locate elsewhere in this broad and expansive land.

. . . I am now spending the final year at Western Seminary, Fremont, Nebraska, amidst the most blessed association; yet anxiously waiting and longing for the day when we can engage in the active work of carrying the Gospel to my brethren, my kinsmen according to the flesh. I am sure readers will excuse this expression of impatience. After one has spent almost three years in practical mission work among the Jews, the life of a student, however pleasant it may be made for him and however necessary he may deem it for his future labors, appears rather drab in comparison with it.

Eddie's last semester at seminary went quickly. Upon graduation, he was approved to receive a call to be pastor of a church. That would allow him to be ordained. When his first trial sermon at a vacant church ended with the congregation choosing someone else, Eddie wondered if his Jewish heritage had kept him out of the pulpit.

Eddie in the Pulpit

Pastor Morentz, who had been Eddie's spiritual mentor, feared that his student might be the victim of prejudice and not used in the church. Pastor Morentz wrote, "It is our prayer that the United Lutheran Church may see fit to use him after he graduates from the seminary even as God has already used him mightily among his own people in Los Angeles."

Eddie prayed that he would receive a call to a vacant church, but for weeks he had no invitations to visit any congregation. Then, at last, the mail brought an invitation to be guest preacher in a church that was looking for a minister. Eddie and Mena were enthusiastic as they prepared to take the train to the city. The church even sent them two railroad passes. That impressed Eddie. Excited about his "trial sermon," Eddie carefully typed out his notes.

Before the train neared the station, Eddie changed into his clerical shirt so that he would look like a minister. He stood at the open door of the car so he could look for the welcoming committee that was to meet them. As the train came in, he spotted a group of people that seemed to be looking for someone, so he waved to them. When Eddie and Mena disembarked, they walked back to where the "welcoming committee" had been waiting, but the group had vanished. Eddie mused about his personal appearance and wondered if his Semitic looks put them off.

Eddie and Mena boarded a local trolley and headed toward the church. They got off a block early, checked the street number and began to walk. As they passed one Jewish store after another, they quickly realized that this was a Jewish community. When they reached the church, it was locked.

What were they to do? Eddie checked all the doors and found one that was open in the basement. There, they set up housekeeping for the night. They had only a little money, but early the next morning Eddie walked to a store and purchased some cereal and milk for breakfast. When people finally started

Eddie, at the pulpit, with the choir at Western Seminary.

17

arriving, Eddie went upstairs and prepared for the service. He set his notes on top of his Bible, then went around meeting the church members. When Eddie returned to the pulpit, his Bible was there, but the notes were gone. At first he panicked, but then he began to preach. He told the people his story of coming to faith in Christ. After the service, the people were cordial, but not really friendly.

Eddie and Mena returned home and waited. They never heard again from the church. Eddie wondered if they were unwilling to have a young Jewish believer as their minister.

A Call From St. Luke in Omaha

Not long after this incident, the first call to ministry came—as an assistant pastor for St. Luke Lutheran Church in Omaha, Nebraska. He would serve with Pastor Oak Ebright. After accepting the call, Eddie had to be ordained. For this he went back to Hollywood Lutheran. The church was filled with friends on his Ordination Day, July 13, 1930. They surprised him with a generous gift of money, including a gold coin. Eddie the carpenter had become "Pastor Eddie Spirer." After ordination, Pastor Eddie and Mena returned to Omaha for his installation at St. Luke.

Eddie enjoyed his work as a visitation pastor. He and Mena seemed to fit in well. St. Luke was building a new church. But there was no hymn board to hold the hymn numbers, so Eddie donned his carpenter's role once more and built a board with lovely wood carving on the top.

On Easter, the pastor's children were given a white rabbit. They kept it in a little pen on their back porch, but the rabbit kept escaping. So Eddie designed and, with his hand tools, built a marvelous rabbit house. It had a gabled roof with a dormer in front. The door and windows had real glass, cut with precision. The kids loved it.

Although the people were friendly and Eddie and Mena were warmly welcomed at St. Luke, the cold winter and the need to shovel the heavy snows

Eddie, with Mena, had received his first calling in 1930 as an assistant pastor for St. Luke Lutheran Church in Omaha, Nebraska.

18

made them homesick for sunny California.
Or was God calling them back for special work in the West?

Launching a Mission Church

One day an unusual invitation came in the mail. A wealthy Los Angeles friend wrote: "Pastor Eddie, my wife and I are going to take a cruise around the world and we will be gone for six months. Would you and Mena come and watch our home while we are away? We do not want it to be empty that long. Of course, we'll take care of all of your expenses, including your trip West."

Eddie and Mena saw this as God providing them a way to get back to California. Eddie resigned from St. Luke, and that spring they drove to Los Angeles. When they arrived at their friend's house, there was a note of welcome and a request to use the new car that was parked in the garage.

Eddie drove up to a ridge that overlooked the San Fernando Valley. From the lookout he could see hundreds of new homes being built. "I looked out and laid claim on that valley for the Lord!"

Eager to launch a mission church, Eddie started ringing doorbells of homes in North Hollywood, which was then the fastest growing area of the valley. He invited hundreds of people to study God's Word. Soon the smiling young minister had a group ready to meet for worship.

Making calls did not cost Eddie money, but renting a room for worship services did; and he had no funds. He found a good meeting room in Duncan Hall, a popular social gathering place—but the rent was ten dollars a month. Eddie asked the Lutheran Church Extension Society for help, but they could only give the mission church $100, which would pay the rent for ten months. After that, they would be on their own.

Eddie designed and built a beautiful hardwood altar and pulpit, and the first service was held on August 2, 1931. Mena taught the first Sunday school class, which had three pupils. The bulletin for Communion Sunday (October 4) reported the first confirmation class taking their stand for Christ. Two months later, on November 29, 1931, St. Matthew's Lutheran Church was organized and welcomed into the California Synod. Eddie chose the name because he thought that Matthew was the "most Jewish" of the Gospels (although three of the four Gospels were written by Jews, and they were all written for Jews).

Their Own Building

The fledgling congregation found property on Camarillo Boulevard in North Hollywood. They raised $1,500 to buy it. Eddie was eager to build, but getting a construction loan during the Depression was very difficult.

Eddie kept pestering the Lutheran Mission Board until a loan was approved. But there was a condition. St. Matthew's had to secure a $1,750 loan from a local bank first: then the board would match the amount. When the banker, who had a reputation for being a tough guy, asked how Eddie would pay the loan, he responded, "You'll get your money every month if I have a can of beans in the house or not." The banker approved the loan.

Of course $3,500 was only a start, hardly enough to buy materials. But Eddie found a way. How did he get the needed materials? He knew that construction sites often had material that was left over and discarded, so he went looking for free lumber. He would tell the work crew at the site that he was building a church and would ask if the wood was available. They often told him to help himself. He soon found enough to start and somehow kept finding enough to keep going. He got many kinds of materials for the new church, even free tile to beautify the building.

Wearing his work clothes, Eddie directed the project. On weekends he recruited the members, young and old, to help. The entire church family was very excited when, on September 16, 1934, they laid the cornerstone.

The kids in the Sunday school wanted to know if there would be "fancy glass" in the church. "No, we can't afford it," Eddie answered. But at home, he started thinking and experimenting with a glass cutter. He drove to a glass firm, went in and asked for the boss. A rather large man was sitting behind a desk. "I started talking about the church," Eddie recalled, "how I needed glass and how the kids in the Sunday school were asking, 'Couldn't we have stained glass for our church?'"

The owner pondered the problem, then offered the glass below wholesale. Eddie thanked the owner, who was Jewish, and headed for the door. "I didn't know we had a synagogue in North Hollywood," called out the owner. Eddie

Three years after being called to St. Matthew's Lutheran Church, North Hollywood, Eddie led his members in building their own church, dedicated in June 1935.

never answered, but just kept going. "That's how we got the stained glass windows. We made them ourselves and the children were very pleased," he said. In the midst of the Depression a newspaper columnist in North Hollywood observed: "Rev. Spirer did not sit down to wait and pray for more prosperous times when they needed their church building. He took off his coat, donned some overalls and went to work to construct the church with his own hands. If it had not been for his personal labor on the building six days a week from early morning until sometimes midnight over the past six months, they would still be meeting in Duncan Hall."

Eddie's Hollywood Connection

In the 1930s the movie industry was booming in Los Angeles. Some of the members of St. Matthew's worked at the studios. Often Eddie would drop by. It seemed as though everyone on the major lots knew Eddie Spirer. In 1934, Katherine Hepburn and Donald Crisp were making a film based on James Barrie's book *The Little Minister*. One day Eddie was watching, standing at the edge of the set, when someone pointed and said, "Look at Pastor Eddie! There's the little minister." Everyone, including Eddie, laughed. The name fit and it stuck. From that day forward, Eddie was The Little Minister. When letters arrived addressed to "The Little Minister, North Hollywood, California," the post office would send them to Pastor Eddie.

St. Matthew's Opens Its Doors

On June 9, 1935, the church built out of throwaways was dedicated. By this time the church had 180 confirmed members, with 250 people attending Sunday school. The Men's Brotherhood had 33 members and there were 48 active members in three women's societies. An active Luther League met weekly, and the church also sponsored a Boy Scout troop. There was a pipe organ and a public address system. The members prepared bulletins and other parish materials on their own printing presses. After nine years, St. Matthew's Lutheran was self-sustaining. Eddie's salary was $3,200 a year, and he and Mena lived in a little house that he had built.

Needing more space, the church purchased an adjoining lot. In the fall of 1940, Eddie and the congregation built a commodious parish building for educational and social activities. Eddie had claimed the whole valley for the Lord, and St. Matthew's was the first fruit of his ministry for Christ the Savior.

The 1941 Parochial Report notes that in ten years Eddie's little mission had grown to 821 baptized members, 477 confirmed members and a Sunday school of 450 people. There were 70 members in the Women's Missionary Society, 40 in the Men's Brotherhood and 140 in the youth group. Their annual budget was $16,200 and they gave $4,478 to missions and benevolence. Their property was valued at $34,000 and they had no indebtedness.

Always a Jew

Sunday Lutheran services always include an Old Testament lesson and a Psalm and many of the hymns are based on Old Testament passages. This pleased Eddie, who was always proud to comment on his Jewish heritage. On Holy Thursday in Holy Week, Eddie often held a Passover seder. He would show how Jesus and his disciples had observed the Jewish feast on the night that Jesus was betrayed. This helped people understand the close relationship between the Jewish faith and the Christian worship service. Eddie always told people that he was a Jew who had accepted the promised Messiah as his Savior and Lord.

One Sunday Eddie extended a special welcome to the Jewish people of the community. Many Kiwanis Club members came, and the church was packed. Eddie preached on the importance of the Jewish heritage to the Christian church, especially the Old Testament prophecies of the coming of the Messiah.

A special fellowship hour, with coffee and refreshments, followed the service. The local newspaper editor was present. He later wrote a column expressing admiration for Eddie and the congregation. St. Matthew's was making an impact on the community!

The population of the San Fernando Valley kept increasing. Many of the newcomers joined St. Matthew's. Harry Rogahn and his family joined in 1948. "We were amazed at the beauty of the sanctuary," said Rogahn. "When we met the pastor, I knew it was for us, especially when he was smaller than I was! I had always wanted to look the preacher straight in the eyes. Now I was looking down at the distinctive hair cut of the man . . . Uncle Eddie, builder of missions, preacher par excellence and, above all, a true son of God."

Through the years many parishioners at St. Matthew's and other churches affectionately called Eddie "Uncle" and Mena "Aunt."

The War Brings Opportunity

While visiting after service on Sunday, December 7, 1941, the people of St. Matthew's heard the news: the Japanese had bombed Pearl Harbor. Everyone began talking excitedly. Eddie called for prayer, asking God to guide the nation. Eddie's prayer quieted the congregation and they went on their way. He always took every aspect of life to God in prayer.

War brought changes everywhere, even in the community around St. Matthew's. Lockheed Aircraft was near the church; soon its huge buildings were covered with camouflage netting.

At Lockheed, Western Technical Training Command started a three-month training school for 300 cadets. When Eddie learned that the school had no chaplain, he volunteered. But they also had no chapel. So St. Matthew's and the local Kiwanis Club donated enough money for Eddie to convert an ordinary square barrack into a chapel, complete with steeple, arches, an altar and pews.

It was dedicated on February 7, 1943. The cadets faithfully came to worship each Sunday.

On Sunday mornings, while Sunday school was in progress at St. Matthew's, Pastor Eddie would drive to Lockheed, lead the chapel service and preach the sermon. Then he would zip back to St. Matthew's in time for the morning service. Hundreds of cadets were touched by the warm witness of Chaplain Eddie. When the school closed in 1944, the commanding officer of the facility expressed his appreciation for the ministry.

The Fruit of Ministry

In addition to the growth at St. Matthew's, there were other fruits of the ministry. Three church members became ministers of the gospel. The first was Christian J. Thearle. He became an air force chaplain. Later he became the head of multicultural ministry in the west for the United Lutheran Church in America (ULCA) and the pastor of St. Mark Lutheran Church in Salem, Oregon.

Thearle first confided in Eddie about his feeling a call into ministry. Together they planned how he would leave Los Angeles City College and enroll at Midland College in Fremont, Nebraska. "But I have no money," Thearle objected to Eddie.

"The Lord will provide," responded the confident pastor.

"Yeah," Thearle agreed, but he really wasn't sure. "That's the way Uncle Eddie was," Thearle later said. "It was no put on. He really believed that, he taught me to believe that, and I guess I've taught other people to believe that."

In World War II, Eddie (left) served as chaplain with cadets at Lockheed, near St. Matthews in North Hollywood. Shown here also are John L. Ross and Captain Nat E. Lewis.

The day that Thearle graduated from Midland, the institution awarded Eddie an honorary doctorate of divinity (Thearle's graduation had nothing to do with Eddie getting the degree).

When Thearle went on to Pacific Lutheran Seminary in Berkeley, California, Eddie kept encouraging him. Whenever Eddie showed up, he would treat Thearle to a first-class meal. Thearle remembers, "Uncle Eddie was an original. There are no copies! He was a deeply spiritual man. He felt deeply and let you know it. He was determined as few men are determined. The Lord Jesus Christ was a personal Lord to Uncle Eddie. When he prayed, you knew they were friends; no, more than that. When he told you, 'The Lord will provide,' it was not to give you a spiritual placebo. He really believed it and the Lord did provide!"

The second member of St. Matthew's to enter the ministry was Kathryn Smithers Lee. Kay and her widowed mother had joined St. Matthew's when they moved to North Hollywood. While attending Hollywood High School, Kay played piano in the Sunday school and taught both Sunday school and Bible school.

Kay married Otis Lee, who, at the time, was in college preparing to go to seminary. Otis remembers hearing Pastor Eddie address a big laymen's dinner meeting at Hollywood Lutheran Church. These men were not real sure about this little Jewish Lutheran pastor, but Eddie soon won their hearts. His string of stories had them laughing so hard they almost fell off their chairs. After telling of his conversion, Eddie challenged the men to witness to their Jewish neighbors.

Eddie and Mena honored on their 25th wedding anniversary, October 30, 1946, at St. Matthews.

After getting married, Otis and Kay served in parishes in Idaho, California, Alaska and North Dakota. They also served a stint as missionaries in Brazil. In 1975, Kay enrolled in Luther Seminary and was ordained in 1979. As a grandmother, she served with her husband in North Dakota, then on the national staff of American Lutheran Church and Evangelical Lutheran Church in America. In "retirement" Kay and Otis now serve as interim pastors in parishes near their home in South Dakota.

The third person to enter the ministry was Roger Rogahn, one of Harry Rogahn's twin sons. The Rogahns were very active in church life, and Harry was Sunday school superintendent. "I guess my parents prayed me into the ministry," says Roger. "They always made it clear that one of their twin sons was to become a minister."

Roger Rogahn studied at Claremont College and Pacific Lutheran Seminary, and he received his Ph.D. from the University of Southern California. He served three parishes in Southern California and, in 1982, was called as director of the Los Angeles Metro Ministry.

All three of those who became pastors from Eddie's church also did graduate work, served in parishes and in special ministries, and held staff positions in their synods.

Eddie Takes On a New Building Project

Eddie's ministry had many dimensions, but it always seemed to come back to building.

For years the California Synod had sought to develop a home for older persons. They had set aside a small fund for the purchase of land, but the dream lay dormant until Dr. James Prince Beasom Jr. spotted a splendid piece of property in Alhambra, California. It had been the winter estate of the legendary James Hill, builder of the Northern Pacific Railroad. Later it became the home of Dominic "The Banana King" Jebbia.

Dr. Beasom, who was synod president at the time, was determined to acquire the property. He wrote out a personal check for $25,000 as a down payment. To do this, he had to mortgage his home. Dr. Beasom brought Eddie to the estate to determine whether it was suitable for use as a home for the aged. A few weeks later, upon a recommendation from Dr. Beasom and Eddie, the annual convention approved the purchase.

Dr. Beasom asked Eddie to serve on the first board of directors for the California Lutheran Home for the Aged (later changed to California Lutheran Homes).

When Eddie had time to inspect the property carefully, he pointed out to Dr. Beasom that not only were the upper floor ceilings too low to meet the state code, but the fire code required the lath plaster walls be replaced with drywall.

"How much is this going to cost?" a surprised Dr. Beasom wanted to know. "The synod has no funds for renovating this property."

Materials alone would have a high price tag, Eddie informed Dr. Beasom. But the Little Minister had an idea: "We could save a lot if we do it with volunteer labor."

Eddie suggested that someone visit churches to recruit volunteer workers

Pastor Eddie with leaders of the Luther League at St. Matthews, 1947.

and ask for donations. Liking the idea, Dr. Beasom asked Eddie to head up the project.

The request really surprised Eddie. After pondering it for a moment, he said he would take on the task. Since this would require Eddie to be away from St. Matthew's during the week, he asked for someone to help with his parish visitation. Dr. Beasom promised to find an assistant.

Everyone Pitches In to Help Eddie

After getting the approval of his church council, Eddie embarked upon a whirlwind tour of churches in the Synod. The Little Minister's enthusiasm was so contagious that soon the synod had the funds and volunteers needed to get started on what was called the Alhambra Home project. Some pastors volunteered to work each week on their day off—everyone wanted to help Eddie!

Eddie studied the plans drawn up and donated by architect Robert Inslee. He bought materials. He lived at the Alhambra Home so he could lay out each day's work and welcome the volunteers. Every morning, he gathered the workers together to pray for guidance and safety.

As the volunteers worked tearing down walls and hauling away debris, putting in drywall and painting, Eddie's energy and endless jokes kept everyone in good spirits. He delighted in reminding them of his Jewish heritage as he teased them: "You folks made my people work as slaves in Egypt, but now I'm going to get even with you. Come on now, let's get this job done!" They laughed at Eddie and worked hard.

Week by week changes were made: the roof was raised, the fireproof walls put in place, other alterations completed. A pastor who was also an experienced plumber volunteered to install additional bathrooms.

Eddie had some close calls, which made some folks wonder if he had a guardian angel watching over him. One day as he was working on a scaffold fifteen feet above the ground, a support broke and Eddie tumbled down. Workers watching him fall held their breath. Fortunately a lattice broke the descent, so Eddie got up, brushed himself off, and went on to the next task. Saturday afternoons were special. Eddie put on a barbecue for all the volunteers. Before long, the renovations were finished, and the Alhambra Home passed the state inspection.

Two thousand guests came to the open house on Sunday afternoon September 14, 1947. On November 1, 1947, Eddie led a service of dedication as the Alhambra Home welcomed its first residents. Among the first 15 guests were retired missionaries and veteran mission pastors of the synod.

Lutherans Need a Church Builder

Meanwhile, St. Matthew's had grown since it was organized in 1931, and so had the synod. Thanks to Eddie, St. Matthew's had an adequate facility. But many other new mission congregations were either crowded in house chapels or worshipping in rented space. After watching Eddie work miracles as a builder at the Alhambra Home, Dr. Beasom wondered if Eddie could build the churches they needed.

The task required a miracle—prohibitively high costs kept new missions from building. The challenge for Eddie was to keep the costs down and get the buildings up. He had been successful with the St. Matthew's and Alhambra projects, so why not on a larger scale? Dr. Beasom came up with a plan and presented it to the synod's executive board. He proposed the creation of a Church Extension Department with Eddie as its head. The board liked the idea, so Dr. Beasom took the plan to the national Board of American Missions which coordinated and financed all of the United Lutheran Church of America mission work.

The Board of American Missions approved the plan and directed their executive, Dr. Zenan Corbe, to extend a call to Eddie to become church extension director in the Southwest. This call put Eddie in a tough situation: he would have to leave the church he built in order to build churches for others. He told Dr. Beasom he would accept the position only if his church voted to release him. The vote at St. Matthew's was unanimous: "No, we will not!" They were far too attached to the Little Minister. Eddie phoned Dr. Beasom with the news of the vote, and he relayed it to the board in New York.

There was only one problem: the board had been so positive Eddie would accept the position that they had already released the news to *Lutheran* magazine. The issue containing the report was already in the mail. Furthermore, the western secretary, Dr. Arthur Knutsen, was on a train coming to visit St. Matthew's to thank the congregation for releasing their pastor.

St. Matthew's members had received their copies of *Lutheran* by the time Dr. Knutsen arrived, and they were furious. Dr. Beasom played peacemaker. "Why can't Eddie do both?" he said. Eddie could spend his weekends at St. Matthew's. During the week he could build mission churches. St. Matthew's would not lose their pastor, they would only "loan" him during the week. To make this plan work the synod would provide an assistant pastor for St. Matthew's to be there during the week. Reassured they would not lose their pastor, St. Matthew's gave their approval. Dr. Beasom had won the day. But now Eddie would have two jobs—and never a day off!

The New Challenge: Eddie as Pastor and Builder

When a reporter from *Valley Life* magazine asked Eddie how he felt about his new challenge, he answered: "I do not consider that church buildings alone are a sufficient reward for the effort put forth to create them. They are only a facility for church congregations to unite in faithful Christian service. The richness and splendor of the church is something that comes with congregational leadership and the warm and inspiring interpretation of the Word. I want to be so fully consecrated to the Lord as to give Him all of myself. Every dime in savings by the grace of God I can effect makes for greater advance of the cause . . . which is the only hope for ushering in 'peace on earth, good will toward men.'"

Knowing Eddie faced a big challenge, Dr. Beasom told him, "Go out and buy the tools and equipment you will need." Eddie soon had a pickup truck with a large California Synod insignia on each door, a concrete power buggy, a 16-inch radial saw, a 10-inch swing saw, three skill saws, two 6-inch mill saws, a jig saw, a band saw and a power sander. Now Eddie was ready.

During one of Eddie's many church construction projects, he inspects a board with a carpenter.

He brought a rare combination of talent and experience to the task. His dedication and long hours of labor won over any skeptics. His enthusiasm was contagious, but what really kept the volunteers coming was his infectious good humor. People loved to work with him. Soon he had four churches under construction and others waiting their turn, so he had to buy additional equipment.

The First Official Project

Eddie's first project was Salem Lutheran in Whittier, California, where David

Robison was pastor. They started work in an orange grove in March 1948 and dedicated a new building in May of the same year. The commercial estimate for building of the church had been $19,600. But Eddie and his crew were able to build the church 12 feet longer than estimated, add a tile floor in the kitchen, build fine oak pews, an altar and the pulpit. They also installed a forced air heater. All this cost just $18,000. The church even had leaded glass windows, which Eddie had taught Pastor Robison to make.

How did they do it? Pastor Robison said, "This project was a self-help project. If Eddie had been named Irving, not Edward, his initials would have spelled 'INSPIRER'! He really inspired our members to participate, and often on Saturday evening we enjoyed one of Eddie's famous barbecues."

On most Sundays Eddie was back at St. Matthew's. He enjoyed preaching and usually gave a report on the progress of the new church buildings. He and Mena still lived in the small house he had built in 1932. Often Eddie did not get home until late Saturday and he had to leave Sunday evening to coordinate the growing number of projects.

A Mission Miracle in San Diego

Former U.S. Navy Chaplain Quentin P. Garman organized Christ Lutheran Church in Pacific Beach (in San Diego) in the summer of 1947. The congregation's first chapel, a small remodeled radio repair shop, was soon packed with people. Pastor Garman turned to Eddie for help.

Christ Lutheran needed to expand quickly, so Eddie enlisted the help of Hans Andersen, a local contractor. When they remodeled the old radio shop, they added a steeple and a cross that made it look like a church, and they built a chapel. The entire job cost only $16,000.

As usual, Eddie found ways to keep the cost low. He spent very little on meals or motels. He slept on the Garmans' davenport so often that their son, Wally, called him Uncle Eddie. Wally liked him because he always found a quarter in Uncle Eddie's pocket. Wally's dad wasn't quite as happy when Eddie woke him up at five in the morning to run the cement mixer! At eight, Eddie and Pastor Garman usually took a break for breakfast, then returned to the building job. Eddie worked hard, and he expected others to do the same.

Working with Eddie, Pastor Garman learned things seminary had not taught him: how to read blueprints, how to lay kitchen tile and how to make stained glass windows. Pastor Garman watched Eddie visit tradespeople and persuade them to make contributions of materials or give discount prices for the new mission church. As Pastor Garman observed Eddie raising money, he learned that the only sin is not asking in the Lord's name for people to respond.

Eddie found a ship's bell in navy surplus and acquired it for the chapel. He thought a former navy chaplain and his shipmates would enjoy hearing a ship's bell again. This was typical of Eddie—he often added a special touch to each new mission church.

On November 25, 1948, the new Christ Lutheran Church building was dedicated. Eddie and Mena were honored as special guests.

Christ Lutheran grew so fast that Eddie returned in 1951 to build an educational unit. Again he organized volunteer labor from the parish and kept costs to a minimum. Wally Garman now had a little brother, Andy, who quickly learned that Uncle Eddie's pocket often contained two quarters.

Help for Northern California

Eddie also helped missions in Northern California. Several of the Bay Area mission pastors had also been recruited by Dr. Beasom. Glen Balsley was at Vallejo, where there was a large navy shipyard and E. Dale Click was at San Mateo. At Vallejo, St. Paul's mission had only a small house chapel. Eddie mobilized the members, many of them skilled shipyard workers who knew how to handle tools. Everyone pitched in. Soon the cornerstone was laid, and before long the new sanctuary was dedicated.

In San Mateo, St. Andrew's Lutheran congregation was waiting for their turn. When the job in Vallejo was done, the members from San Mateo picked up the scaffolding. In the following weeks, Eddie did for St. Andrew's what he had done for so many other congregations.

But they almost didn't get a fireplace. Eddie told the people in San Mateo that they could not afford one. However, the people in San Mateo really wanted that fireplace. So their pastor borrowed an idea from Eddie. Pastor Click was on a fund-raising campaign in San Diego when he met a brick contractor. He persuaded that contractor to come to San Mateo to lay brick for the fireplace and promised to carry the cement (hod) for the contractor. The contractor agreed, and Pastor Click hauled the hod for all three stories of the fireplace.

Said Pastor Click: "He [Eddie] motivated lay people and pastors to do much of the labor, trained lay people and pastors in building . . . demonstrated skills in getting materials and sub-contractors and conducted himself as a Christian gentleman, an ardent laborer (in overalls much of the time), and he never asked anybody to do something he wouldn't do.

"Congregations came closer together in those days because they worked together under a little guy who followed the 'great Carpenter's command.' In those days, mission pastors wore overalls as much as clerical robes."

More than $30,000 Saved

Eddie helped a church in Altadena, near Los Angeles. Christ the Good Shepherd was worshipping in a house chapel. The low bid to build their new church was $77,000. Eddie built it for $42,000! No wonder they thought that he was a miracle worker.

When the church was completed, the house chapel became the parsonage for Pastor Howard Lenhardt and his family. One day Eddie noticed a crack running through the counter top in the kitchen. He asked why it hadn't been fixed. Pastor Lenhardt explained that the building committee told him there were no funds. Without a word, Eddie lifted his sledge hammer high and let it drop, smashing the counter to pieces. Eddie grinned and said, "Well, now they will have to replace it." Eddie put in the new counter, and, for years, Lenhardt chuckled every time he looked at it.

Next to the church in Altadena lived a sculptor named Nishan Toor. Eddie discovered that Toor had no studio, so he struck a deal with him. Eddie would build Toor a studio if Toor would create some pieces of art for the church. Toor was delighted at the offer. He made two carvings, the altar wood carving and, for the entrance to the church, a lunette carving of Christ the Good Shepherd. And Eddie built a fine studio for Nishan Toor.

Altadena's Pastor Lenhardt remembers this about Eddie: "If a problem ever came up Eddie would often quote a verse from the Psalms, one that fit perfectly. As he kept us working, he frequently quoted the Bible verses and at the same time teased and joked with us."

Christ the Good Shepherd Lutheran's attendance more than doubled in the years after the building was complete, and the Sunday school went to two sessions.

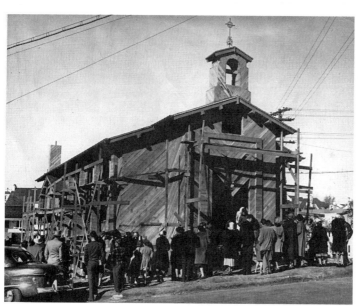

One of Eddie's many building projects taking shape in the early '50s.

31

Three Steps to Building a Church

After completing a few projects, Eddie soon developed a system. Each project had three steps. Step One was a visit by Eddie to discuss the needs of the church. Some new missions owned land but were meeting in rented space. A few older churches wanted their existing building enlarged or remodeled. Some congregations had outgrown their chapel and needed to build a larger sanctuary, but the contractors' bids were beyond their budget. That is when they usually would beg Eddie to help them.

Step Two was the preparation of plans for the project. The national church required that a long-range site plan be prepared before any first unit could be built. This study would reserve space for second and third phases and for parking and other needs, avoiding costly mistakes. An architect, usually Bob Inslee, would prepare the plans that Eddie would follow.

Step Three was the supervision of the project by Eddie. He often had three or four projects going at one time. To keep things moving, he used a team of qualified carpenters on each site to guide the construction. Eddie kept an eye on each team. In Reno and a few other places he used a local contractor who worked closely with him. For all projects, Eddie purchased materials in large quantities, thus saving the churches hundreds of dollars. He persuaded members to do as much work as they possibly could. Knowing it would keep the costs down, members gladly helped.

A few churches chose not to use Eddie. Pastor John Stump's congregation in La Canada heard his presentation, but when Eddie suggested they save money by eliminating a fireplace, they lost interest. La Canada had planned carefully and knew just what they wanted. So they kept their fireplace and used a local contractor, even though going that way was more expensive.

Goodbye to St. Matthew's

As Eddie gave progress reports on the building projects to the people back at St. Matthew's, they could see how much he loved to build these mission churches. But in time Eddie realized that he could not keep up the pace he had set; and he knew that he had to ask again to be released.

One Sunday he told his congregation, "If you want me continue to do this [work both jobs], I will. But I am convinced that God has called me to help these mission churches get their new buildings. This schedule is killing me; I cannot keep this up."

The members saw that he was right. They reluctantly voted to accept his resignation. Then they elected him pastor emeritus!

While serving at St. Matthew's, Eddie had baptized 330 people, confirmed 174, performed 405 weddings and conducted 143 funerals. While holding down both jobs, Eddie had completed 15 churches in two years. Now he could focus solely on the building projects.

How Eddie Worked His Miracles

Eddie worked closely with Dr. Beasom. Each mission church that was planning to build had to have a funding campaign and get pledges. When these pledges were in, the Board of Missions would advance a construction loan and often help by giving a second mortgage at low interest. This way, the building project could start immediately.

Getting the proper building permits from city hall was part of Eddie's job. Since he was a contractor, he knew exactly how to get approval for the drawings and care for all of the necessary paperwork.

As a new church was getting started, Eddie usually spent a week there to get the permits and explain the program to the church members. He often preached on Sunday to encourage the people to volunteer for simple tasks and help save money.

On the job Eddie was the boss! He hired local subcontractors, purchased material at wholesale rates and saw that the materials arrived at the job site. When a new building was completed, Eddie had it inspected immediately so that the congregation could move right in.

Eddie directed and helped build the first projects, but as the program expanded he relied more and more on a team of trusted carpenters on each building site. He monitored the progress by phone and with visits.

What About Standards?

Eddie's amazing construction record astonished everyone—well, almost everyone. Some people who didn't understand his methods suggested that the new churches were not well built and might not stand up for long. ULCA President Franklin Clark Fry wanted to know if the buildings were up to code. He was told that all the buildings were approved by the Committee on Church Architecture. And savings were achieved because:

- Eddie Spirer worked for a "trifling amount" of personal compensation. He was woefully underpaid.

- Eddie Spirer got good prices for materials.

- A California-type construction was used with "free interpretation of plans and specifications."

Eddie didn't agree! He didn't think he was an underpaid contractor. He believed God had called him to serve as a carpenter-builder and he loved to save the Lord's money. Churches got a good deal because Eddie was working for the Lord, not for money. And he was working about 18 hours a day, with no days off.

Wayne Pfundstein, synod comptroller and a neighbor of Eddie's, handled the finances of the program. The Department of Church Extension was a sepa-

33

rate account, and its work was closely monitored. All bills for supplies were channeled through the synod, and Pfundstein handled all the salary checks for the staff, upon Eddie's authorization. Eddie had a network of suppliers and subcontractors who knew him and were glad to help his projects succeed. At first, Eddie's salary was only $200 a month and was paid by a special grant from the Board of American Missions. Eddie kept personal expenses very low, and he never had to buy a car because an auto dealer who admired him gave him a new one each year.

One way Eddie kept expenses down was to purchase lumber by the freight car load directly from the mill. When lumber arrived in Los Angeles, Eddie and his crew would cull out odds and ends, finding ways to use them. Then they would truck the lumber to the various construction sites. He had wholesale contracts for doors, windows and everything needed to build a church.

Sometimes Pfundstein went along when Eddie visited major suppliers. Negotiations would always start in the owner's office, where Eddie would informally describe this new church program as the Lord's work. He would go on to speak of his desire to save all of the Lord's dollars he could. Then Eddie would lead in prayer, asking for the Lord's guidance. Only then would the building needs be outlined and a price discussed. Many dealers offered special prices!

Making the Right Connections

In Richmond, California, when constructing Grace Church, Eddie bought so much lumber from one lumber yard that he and the owner became good friends. Later, as he was preparing to build a church in Honolulu, Eddie visited his friend in Richmond. He explained that he needed prime redwood lumber that was termite-resistant. The owner had grown so fond of Eddie that he donated all the redwood. This saved the Honolulu congregation hundreds of dollars.

A Bold Suggestion

In Fresno, at Trinity Lutheran, an older congregation led by Phil Jordan was ready to expand. Eddie was asked to evaluate their plans to remodel their downtown building. His recommendation shocked them. "By no means should you put more money into this old building that has termites," Eddie said. "You need more land because you have no parking. Move out and find a larger lot on the growing edge of Fresno!"

After they recovered from the shock, Trinity saw the wisdom of his suggestion. They sold their property for $25,000 and bought a ten acre site on the edge of town. It was so far out that people often called this new church site "Jordan's folly." But the growth of the church proved that Eddie had been right. Today Trinity's $2,500,000 structure is used for a creative ministry.

Eddie's Other Projects

The Swedish Lutheran churches (Augustana Lutherans) also requested Eddie's help. He built five churches for them, including ones in Alameda, San Francisco and Fresno.

Eddie helped other Lutheran ministries. Quentin Garman had started and directed a youth camping program. The program expanded, and the synod called Jack Foerster as its director. Foerster also served as pastor of the First Lutheran Church in Redlands. A new site was needed for a year-round camp program. In 1957, Foerster's organist surprised him by offering to sell her prime orchard land near Yucaipa at an excellent price. The synod bought it, but now they needed some buildings. Once again Eddie came to the rescue and at minimal cost built a lodge and two housing units. Thanks to Eddie, the synod now had a youth camp and conference center.

In 1953, Eddie was back at Alhambra for another project. The home for the aged was filled: now it needed an infirmary. Eddie took on the task, serving as the contractor for the new six-bed facility, which he finished in 1954.

By 1956 even more space was needed. It was decided that Alhambra should double in size. Plans were made to build a new wing of 25 modern living units. Eddie was ready. He directed all of the work and the addition was completed and dedicated in 1957.

During construction of the new wing, Eddie began to think that someday he might like to retire—"maybe." He struck a deal with the board. He would build an extra cottage at his own expense, using leftover lumber from the construction job. Someday he and Mena would move into the "Eddie Spirer Cottage." Years later, Mena spent her last years in that cottage.

A Miracle for Grace Lutheran

When Grace Lutheran Church in Richmond, California, planned to build a new church across the street from the civic center, they called Eddie. He studied the site and Bob Inslee's plan. Then, as usual, he asked the members of the congregation to help. However, a problem came up. Eddie feared they might not be able to acquire all of the materials they needed. On his way up from Los Angeles, where he had checked on some other projects, Eddie had an unusual experience. He explains:

> I needed structural steel for the ceiling beams for Grace Church, and that had me worried. Steel was hard to get, and I did not have the "points" required at that time. When I got back to the San Francisco airport I got on the bus to go over to Richmond. As we went along South San Francisco I don't know what hit me but I had a sudden urge to get off the bus! Anyway, I got off the bus and started walking along the street. I noticed the firms that were in that area, and ahead of me

was a large steel fabrication business. I decided to walk in, and when inside I asked the secretary who the boss was. She replied, "It's Mr. Hansen." I asked if he was in and she said he was and that he would see me. As I walked in I remember saying to myself, "With a name like Hansen, he just may be a Lutheran." I was welcomed into his office, and right away I began to tell my story of our work building churches and the big project we had over in Richmond. He listened with interest and did not stop me when I told him we needed some steel beams for the ceiling of the church but that our money was in short supply.

Imagine my surprise when he answered, "Well, I think we can give you the beams that you need, but we cannot deliver them to you. You will have to see that they are picked up and delivered to the site." I thanked him and told him we certainly could manage that. As I left I understood why God had led me to get off that bus and take a walk.

Later we found a member in Grace Church who had access to a large truck to move the steel to the site at the proper time. After we had the material on the site and had a large crane ready to move the beams up into place we had a surprise visit from the steel workers' union. Apparently someone had alerted the union official in Richmond, and all of a sudden we had pickets there to register a protest. They demanded that the work be stopped because it was not being done with union labor. I took them aside and introduced myself and told the story of our work. That we had prayed to God for His help in getting this church up and that much of the labor was being done by members as volunteers. I was a minister but had been in construction in my early life and was an architect, and God had called me to supervise these new mission church buildings. As I was talking it was very interesting to see the change that came over these men. I was surprised, for not only did they change, but the union official offered to come and donate a day of labor himself to help us complete the project. It had happened once more! Time and time again I learned that God will provide. Every time we had a need we just prayed and God would lead us and guide us and people would come and help.

A remarkable total of 8,000 hours of volunteer labor was contributed by members and friends in the construction of the $200,000 church. Not only had Eddie kept within the budget, but there was enough money left to buy new pews.

Grace Lutheran was dedicated on December 14, 1952. One more of Eddie's spires held the cross of Christ high in the heart of a city. In the bulletin, Pastor Milus Bonker, commended Eddie. "His is a great ministry for the

Lord as he guides congregations in the erection of Houses of Prayer throughout the Synod," he wrote. "God has wrought a miracle in providing a church and furnishings far beyond our expectations at the beginning of the construction program. Dr. Spirer's leadership has enabled us to use the Lord's money to the greatest advantage and we stand amazed and humbly grateful at what has been accomplished."

Transforming a Garage into a Seminary!

Lutherans needed a seminary on the West Coast to train pastors. In a joint venture, the California Synod and the Pacific Synod in the Northwest agreed to establish a theological seminary in Berkeley. They secured two large estates on eight acres. Classes were to open in September of 1952. In July seminary president Charles B. Foelsch arrived at the campus. He quickly determined that the school needed three additional faculty offices and another classroom, but funds for construction were limited. Dr. Foelsch called Eddie.

Dr. Foelsh showed Eddie the two-level, six-car garage on campus. "Could you remodel this?" he asked.

Eddie looked it over, took measurements and told Dr. Foelsch, "Sure I can, so don't worry. I'll draw the plans and get the materials, and this will be my gift to our new seminary."

On the upper floor Eddie designed a large classroom and on the lower level three faculty offices. When Dr. Harry Mumm, the first professor, arrived in August 1952, he found the boxes of books and other effects he had shipped ahead stacked outside the lower level garage. Eager to move into his new quarters, he offered to help Eddie with the remodeling job. They made quite a pair. Dr. Mumm stood at six feet, four inches. Eddie was just five feet tall.

First they installed the framing, then the flooring over the concrete base of the garage. The middle space on the lower level was where Mumm's office would be. There they found a lubrication pit with steps going down—there was even some oil in the drain tanks. They just covered it up.

Other people came to help put drywall on the framing, build fronts for the offices and put in the doors, windows, bookshelves and a furnace. Before long everything was done except the floor tiling. Eddie phoned neighboring St. Michael's Lutheran Church and asked them to lay the linoleum tile on both levels. The pastors recruited a work force, including Larry Varblow, whose son was planning to enter seminary the next fall.

Preparing the Chapel Furniture

The chapel services would be held in the large living room in the lower estate. When Eddie learned they had no chapel furniture, he told Dr. Foelsch not to worry. He promised to make some when he went home. Eddie kept his promise. A lovely walnut altar and lectern arrived before the first week of classes. Many others besides Eddie helped prepare for the seminary opening. The Women's Auxiliary, which had been organized for a year, provided all of the furnishings.

The opening service was held in the outdoor chapel on a Sunday afternoon in 1952. The next day classes began and the first chapel service was held. Dr. Mumm went forward to read the Scripture lessons. As he stood there towering over the lectern, he realized that Eddie had made it, not for a six-foot, four-inch professor, but for a "little minister." But the lectern was used for years, until a new chapel was built.

A Call From Hawaii

Eddie was working on a project in San Diego when he received a call from Pastor Hamme in Honolulu, Hawaii. The state had purchased their church building and the church needed to relocate. Would he help?

"I went over and made arrangements for the old hotel on their new site to be torn down while I was finishing in San Diego," Eddie recounts. "The mission board also wanted me to construct other churches while I was there, so I visited these and went back."

Mena went with Eddie, and she really enjoyed those weeks in the islands. But soon after they arrived Pastor Hamme became so ill that he had to resign and return to the mainland. Now Eddie was both pastor and builder. Although it kept him very busy, Eddie enjoyed the opportunity to again preach on a regular basis.

As usual, Eddie invited the members to help, and many responded. One of the members, Art Hansen, recalls what drew him to the Little Minister:

I had been a member of the Lutheran Church of Honolulu for over a year. . . I was anything but enthusiastic about taking an active part in building the church. However, I soon found myself on planning committees, in fund-raising groups, painting (I don't even do this at home—I hate painting!) and laying tiles. In fact, one Saturday when we were down with a few people, Eddie asked me to help stain the beams in the ceiling. I forgot that I get dizzy when I'm even five feet off the ground, and when I got up there I froze. They had to tear me off to get me down. That is the power he had over me.

In my early days as a church member, he took me under his wing and proved to me the great power of faith and what it meant in a person's life. I am afraid that if he had fed me a lot of theology at that time, I might have walked away. He proved not only to me but to everyone that a Christian life and a belief in God is not a sober and drab life, but one filled with hope and a real bright look at the future. He has been around to help me whenever I needed him, and he has never let me feel

sorry for myself. His criticism has been appreciated as much as
his love.

Life-Changing Advice

During the time he was working on the church, Art Hansen lost his job with
a wholesale food operation. His boss became terminally ill and decided to
close the business. What should Art do? His wife, Jennie, and Eddie felt he
had a rare opportunity to go into business for himself. Art hesitated, noting
that he had no capital and had never managed a business. Joining hands with
Art and Jennie, Eddie prayed about the matter: "Dear Lord, my friend is scared
to death. He's lost his job and he thinks it's the end of the world. His wife
and I want him to go into business, and if he does, we'll make a covenant that
he'll run it honestly and ethically, with fair treatment to everybody. And he
wants an answer by Tuesday. Amen."

Art accepted Eddie's encouragement and got started right away. On
April 1, 1952, A. H. Hansen Sales, Ltd. opened in a rented office and with just
$900. Jennie took care of the office work. Art soon had his first two accounts:
a West Coast meat supplier gave him an $80,000 line of credit, and a Midwest
poultry firm did the same.

Without a warehouse, without a sales force, and without a company track
record, Art began calling on hotels, markets and restaurants offering frozen
meat and poultry. He handled only high-quality merchandise. Although it was
costly, the tourist industry offered a ready-made market. The business did well
and Eddie's prayer was answered. By April 1, 1972, the company's 20th
anniversary, they were doing $8 million of business annually. They had a
profit-sharing program for their 25 multiracial employees. Art and Jennie
Hansen invited Eddie back to the islands almost every year for a holiday, providing him with a first-class plane ticket. They put him up in a fine hotel on
the beach. Eddie basked in the red-carpet treatment.

In the Pulpit Again

Eddie was an effective pastor while the new church in Honolulu was under
construction. The church welcomed new members, and Eddie baptized three
former Buddhists. The other church-building projects in Hawaii were also
coming along. At Waianae a quonset hut was modified into a sanctuary.

Eddie joined the Kiwanis Club. One Kiwanian owned a concrete brick
company. One day he talked about all the hard work Eddie was doing and
offered sympathy. Eddie said, "No, don't do that. Go home and give the steel
and concrete to help me finish this job as it should be done." The man liked
Eddie so much that he gave him the materials.

When the sanctuary of the Lutheran church in Honolulu was completed, it
was dedicated with a festive celebration.

After Eddie's year in Hawaii, the synod, at its annual convention, might have expected a more detailed report. But Eddie kept true to his reputation as a man of deeds, not words. His report was as follows:

The year of 1953 by the help of God gave your Division of Church Extension its best opportunity of service for Christ. Eleven months of the year your director spent in the construction of the Lutheran Church of Honolulu and St. Paul's, also in Honolulu.

The sacrifice of living away from home was amply compensated by the privilege of serving our downtown church as interim pastor. The grace of God enabled us to weld together this congregation into a working unit for Christ. In addition to erecting a beautiful $125,000 edifice, 38 accessions including the baptism of three former Buddhists were the fruitage of your department's labor.

St. Paul's construction consisted of a two-story concrete and block building with a well-appointed small chapel and classrooms.

It is the hope of this department that the support of the Synod and the guidance of the Holy Spirit may grant us the privilege and opportunity of further advance for Christ.

Eddie's Largest Project
First Lutheran Church in Glendale, California, was Eddie's largest project. It tested all of his training, experience and skills. Synod President James Beasom had once been pastor of this church. So had Dr. Carl Tambert, who would later be a synod president. Both were present for the laying of the cornerstone.

As Eddie was directing the construction of the Glendale church, which filled an entire city block, he was also coordinating the building of churches in Phoenix, San Fernando and Riverside. By this time, many of the churches he had previously worked on had grown so much that they needed expansion.

In 1957, a Los Angeles Times reporter interviewed Eddie about his ten years of church-building activity. Eddie admitted, in the interview, that he would rather have his own church than build churches for others. He lamented being pulled away from individuals time and again. "I feel I am at my best when I have personal contact with the members of a church," he said. "I look forward to the day when I will have my own congregation again."

Honors for Eddie
Eddie Spirer had provided first units for many new missions, larger buildings for a number of older churches and new institutions for the synod. Realizing that most emergency needs had been met, in 1958 the synod

executive board closed the church extension program. At the convention that year, Eddie was honored as "Church Builder of the Synod." Fifty-four churches had been constructed through Eddie Spirer's program.

Dr. Carl Tambert presented Eddie with an impressive book of letters from national leaders and pastors of the churches he had helped build in California, Arizona, Nevada and Hawaii (see Appendix A for a sampling of these letters). Along with the book, Eddie and Mena received a gift of $1500.

In a way, the presentation was Eddie's retirement banquet. But at 63 he didn't go home to live a life of leisure or even enjoy some well-earned rest. He accepted a call to serve as interim pastor in Redding and nearby Central Valley in Northern California.

Eddie the Peacemaker

Synod leaders asked Eddie to encourage the two congregations to merge and form one strong church. The members resisted. For six months Eddie served both congregations, leading two services each Sunday. He did persuade them, however, to have one confirmation class for the young people. And he had them come together for fellowship dinners. For these he baked apple pies, which everyone loved. Soon the congregations became better acquainted. Eddie suggested to the confirmation class that it would be better to form one

Synod Director Carl Bell presents a book full of letters of appreciation and a $1500 check to Eddie and Mena at the 1958 convention of Synod, marking completion of his post as Director of Church Extension. In 10 years he oversaw the construction of 54 buildings.

Each year in Holy Week, Eddie conducted traditional Passover on Holy Thursday.

strong congregation. The students talked with their parents, encouraging them to change their minds. Before long the two churches approved a merger.

The new, united Redding congregation called a full-time pastor, and it was time for Eddie to move on. And move he did. He kept serving as interim pastor for 18 years. There were stops in Altadena, Fresno, Long Beach and Hawaii. He loved being a pastor.

Interim Pastor in Southern California

Eddie and Mena still lived in the small house Eddie had built while they were at St. Matthew's. Mena, suffering from severe arthritis, seldom went with Eddie on his interim assignments. When he was home, Eddie prepared meals for her. He made enough so that she would have meals while he was away. When out of town, Eddie phoned Mena every day to make sure she was all right.

Then St. Michael's Lutheran Church in nearby Sun Valley, California, asked Eddie to serve as interim pastor. The offer appealed to him because it meant he could be with Mena each night. The members of St. Michael's responded so well to Eddie's ministry that the church began to grow. It wasn't long before congregation members discontinued their outside search for a permanent pastor and asked Eddie to fill the post. He accepted and served as pastor in Sun Valley from 1973 to 1976.

Mena's Long Illness

In November of 1972, while Eddie was serving at St. Michael's, Mena's arthritis became so severe that it became apparent that she needed special care. That was when she moved to "Eddie's Cottage" at the Alhambra Home. She was very comfortable there and received the care she needed. Eddie visited her regularly until her death on January 22, 1974.

Eddie mourned the loss of Mena. But he kept busy caring for the church at Sun Valley. Since he no longer made the 45-minute-a-day trip to Alhambra, he had more time to care for the sick and shut-ins.

They Won't Let Him Retire

The church kept growing, and so did Eddie's reputation. In August 1973, reporter Natalie Hall wrote about the 78-year-old pastor in a feature story. She called him a "kooky, sawed-off, fun-loving, Bible-toting, joke-cracking" pastor who liked to talk to strawberries because he thought it made them grow better. Hall also identified him as a "pastor, mission organizer, church builder, retired minister, interim supply pastor" who had touched thousands of lives.

The article went on to note that kids loved Eddie—even dogs followed him around. "Grown-ups like him so much they won't let him retire," she wrote. "He quips, 'I have only one real asset. I love people.'"

Marie Anne Carranza, chairperson of the church Sharing and Caring Committee, told Hall that she saw a difference at St. Michael's since Eddie Spirer arrived. "We laugh in our church now," Miss Carranza said.

Fun was high on Eddie's agenda. "Some people, when they go to church, think they have to put on a big sour puss to make people think they're sincere," he was quoted as saying. "Well, I like to have fun here. I've had fun all my life. It's so easy not to be a sour puss."

Bagel Gospel and Jelly Roll Ministry

The article mentioned Eddie's homemade jelly rolls. These were quickly becoming a tradition at St. Michael's. Every Saturday night Eddie would bake two jelly rolls, cut them in half and have four to give out on Sunday morning. He would give them to visitors or to members celebrating an anniversary.

The congregation grew to love Eddie. On the forty-fifth anniversary of his ordination they honored him with a special dinner. One Christmas they gave him a brand-new car. In order to see out the front window, he had to sit on the Los Angeles telephone directory.

Besides baking apple pies and jelly rolls, Eddie liked to make special dishes for the people he would visit, especially the sick and shut-ins. On these visits, Eddie was often accompanied by Marie Carranza, who headed many committees, including the one that oversaw visitation. A widow, she had moved to Los Angeles from New England via San Diego. Eddie and Marie enjoyed being together.

Hawaiian Church Seeks Eddie's Help

Settled in quite comfortably at St. Michael's, at 80 years of age, Eddie was shocked when he read the letter. It came from Lihue Lutheran Church on the island of Kauai in Hawaii. They wanted him to be their pastor.

Wanting to check out the opportunity, Eddie phoned his friend Art Hansen, who said, "Come on over." After a visit with the Hansens in Honolulu, Eddie flew to Lihue. He preached on Sunday and took a good look at the situation.

"To start with, the old church building was not in good shape," he said. "Some of the stained-glass windows were broken, some glass had fallen out and you couldn't match this glass because it had come from Germany. The weeds around the church needed cutting, too. There was a lot of work to do. Eddie told them, "Frankly, I think you need a younger man!" With that, he went back to Sun Valley. The members at St. Michael's were relieved; they had feared that they might lose their pastor.

But Lihue just would not give up! The members kept phoning Eddie and sending him letters. Finally Bishop Lloyd Burke asked Eddie to "go back and take another good look at the congregation." Eddie agreed to do this.

He stayed in the parsonage this time. It had no furniture except for a bed. "When the members brought in some food that night," he said, "we all sat on the floor, enjoyed a good meal and had a fine time. Still, when I went to bed I was not convinced that God was calling me to Lihue."

The next day a member of the congregation, a woman, asked Eddie to go with her to visit someone who had not been in church for a long time. He liked making calls, so off they went. "A lady came to the door," Eddie recounted, "but she did not invite us in. I quickly sent up a prayer, 'Lord, I just want to reach that woman!' The woman began to talk and behind her, listening, was her little girl. Then a strange thing happened. After a moment that little girl looked up and said, 'Momma, this little man—I like him!' That melted her mother, and from then on she was very friendly. I realized that I had asked God to help me reach one person, but God helped me reach two!"

That started the wheels moving in Eddie's mind. Maybe there was a mission field in Lihue. Maybe God was calling him here.

Eddie Accepts the Call to Hawaii

Back in Sun Valley, Eddie vacillated. But God got his attention. Eddie explained: "I seemed to hear a voice, 'Eddie, you only want to go where you want to go!' For me, that was it! I knew God was calling me to Lihue!"

He broke the news to the members at St. Michael's at the annual barbecue. They were disappointed, but accepted that it was God's will.

When preparing for the new call, Eddie wrote the following letter to Lihue church member Catherine Lo:

A number of things affected my change of heart concerning Lihue. Your letter that appealed to my heart as well as the still small voice that has kept me stirred up and just refuses to forget Lihue, so I am coming.

The spiritual advance of the Kingdom will largely depend on my becoming a full part of the community. Do you agree? Lihue is a tremendous challenge and I covet the opportunity to be used of the Lord to accomplish His will on the island. I only hope I will not be a disappointment to Him.

I would need additional time to dispose of my home, etc. I do plan to ship my car and furniture and will try to interest Synod in helping with this cost. I must burn all my bridges behind me or I could feel it is still on a temporary basis.

As to the parsonage, I am a man of modest need, though my home is a long cry from the condition of the Lihue parsonage. Use your own judgment as to color. I will be happy if it is clean and quiet.

Eddie did as he promised in the letter and headed off to Kauai, ready for a new adventure! One special friend, Marie Carranza, was quite disappointed when he left. Eddie and Marie kept in touch by mail and by telephone.

Eddie quickly became a part of the community. What happened in the next few years would have been amazing for a young pastor. Soon the Little Minister with the infectious smile and good humor was known all over the island. He regularly visited ailing church members who were in the hospital. His warm spirit encouraged everyone he met. His visits and prayers touched many patients, not just his own members. The nurses and doctors soon became his friends, too. He easily made friends with the other clergymen on the island. But he faced a huge task. His little historic church was infested by termites and desperately needed a major renovation.

Restoring the Church in Lihue

Catherine Lo, historian of the Lihue church, later wrote that the church was in need of restoration on two levels: physical and spiritual. The task seemed impossible—at least it would have seemed so to most pastors. When Eddie arrived in 1976, the Lihue church was 90 years old, just nine years older than he was. But Eddie plunged in. He was determined, his energy seemingly unlimited. The church historian praised him: "He has proved time and again to his people that indeed with God all things are possible."

The church council had asked local contractors for estimates. To reinforce the foundation and restore the quaint beauty of the structure was going to cost at least $50,000 and take five years of hard work—a mammoth undertaking for a tiny congregation. That didn't daunt Eddie. In fact, he wanted the project to be even larger. Eddie proposed all sorts of renovations that had not originally been considered. And he insisted that the project include the parish hall and the parsonage.

The project became a community effort, with Lutherans and non-Lutherans working side by side. People from Kauai, Oahu and the mainland contributed gifts of time, skills, materials and money. Everything except the steeple was touched in some way. The 24 wooden posts that held up the floor of the church were replaced with steel supports. The underpinnings were imbedded in concrete. "No food for termites," Lo wrote. Seven of the nine full-size windows were releaded and missing pieces replaced. Four that could not be restored were replaced with stained-glass sections that depict Bible stories. These were donated by a church in Beverly Hills, California, that Eddie had built two decades earlier.

Colorful Touches

There was a new spirit in the church at Lihue and pews were full. Eddie loved the people at Lihue, and they knew it.

Either Saturday night or early Sunday morning Eddie would bake jelly rolls. This was a tradition he had started years earlier. Why jelly rolls? Someone had told Eddie they were the hardest things in the world to make. Never one to back away from a dare, he had set to it and rolled out the dough. And the jelly rolls had come out very nicely. Eddie's mother had always had some tea and cookies for visitors who came to their house—even the mailman. So, in a way, Eddie was carrying on a family tradition.

Eddie would always make two jelly rolls, then cut them in half so he would have a gift for four people. "When time came for the announcements, I would have some fun," Eddie explained. "I called it 'my hour with my people.' I would bring news to their attention, then give out those jelly rolls for some special event like an anniversary or for some visitors. They liked it!"

Always a pioneer, Eddie launched a new liturgical tradition for the churches in Hawaii. He asked that worship stoles be made of the colorful Hawaiian fabrics that he liked so much. As a special gift, Maxine Pascual and her daughter, Sally Rasay, bought the material and sewed not only the stoles but also paraments for the altar and pulpit. When Father Ernest Claes, the Roman Catholic priest, was honored on his ordination anniversary, Eddie presented him with a Hawaiian stole. Methodist pastor Ray Sasaki followed by wearing colorful stoles on Oahu, spreading what has now become a liturgical legacy of Eddie's in Hawaii.

Eddie and Marie

Marie Carranza visited Lihue a few times. The two had grown close, and she hoped he would propose marriage. He didn't, so she decided that nothing would happen. But she let Eddie know how she felt. Eddie answered that he was busy with the church renovation project, and she understood. For months they exchanged letters and ran up huge phone bills. But Eddie never even hinted at a wedding.

The building project was almost complete, and big plans were being made for a festive day of dedication. The national bishop, James Crumley, had been invited along with California Bishops Stanley Olson and Lloyd Burke.

Before the dedication, Eddie had to make a trip to California. While he was there, he visited Marie. She didn't suspect anything was afoot. Eddie casually told her, "By the way, when they rededicate the church, the bishop said he would have our wedding!" Marie was stunned. When she recovered, she said that that was fine with her!

The Wedding in Hawaii

The dedication of the renovated church was to be at the Sunday service and the wedding one hour later. Marie feared that the wedding might be lost in the excitement over the dedication. But she needn't have worried; everything went nicely.

There was a technicality about who could conduct the wedding service. At the last minute, Eddie realized that the national bishop could not perform the wedding because only resident clergy were authorized to do that in Hawaii. But Eddie had an idea. Some weeks earlier, he had missed his flight from Honolulu to Kauai. He stood at the gate watching his plane take off without him. Then he overheard someone say that the governor's plane, which was parked nearby, was preparing to take off for Kauai. Eddie strolled out to that plane, stood with the governor's party and got on the plane with them. After they took off, Eddie introduced himself to the governor. He had heard of

Eddie and his wife, Marie, in Waikiki, boat to Fern Grotto for a wedding.

Eddie. The governor told Eddie to call on him if he could ever be of help.

Eddie remember and telephoned the governor. He explained the situation and the governor gave a special authorization for Bishop Crumley to conduct the wedding. Eddie knew God would work things out—He always did!

The lovely wedding ceremony was held right on schedule.

Bishop Crumley was assisted by Bishop Olson and Bishop Burke, each wearing a colorful Hawaiian stole. Eddie and Marie wore maile leis, which are worn for very special occasions.

Bishop Burke later recalled that Eddie was a bit impatient; he even tried to help with the ceremony. "He didn't even trust the national bishop," said Burke, "but he was married anyway."

Art and Jennie Hansen hosted the wedding dinner at the Kauai Surf Hotel. Eddie and Marie did not take a honeymoon. The bride noted, "Where could we have gone? We were already in paradise!"

Eddie reached another milestone while in Lihue: the fiftieth anniversary of his ordination as a minister of the gospel. On July 27, 1980, a festive dinner was held to mark the occasion. The Lihue congregation prepared a slide presentation titled, "This Is Your Life!"

Still Busy at Eighty-five

At eighty-five, Eddie was still busy leading worship, visiting the sick and participating in community activities. When people revealed a heartache or talked about a burden, he would join hands and say a prayer. One couple came to Eddie after their son wrote and admitted that he had a problem with alcohol and was attending AA meetings. Eddie, who was never afraid to ask specific requests of God, closed his prayer with the couple saying, "Lord, send him a friend to help him in this difficult time." A few days later the parents exuberantly told Eddie that their son had phoned to report that one of his co-workers also attended the AA meeting. The two were going to work together to overcome their problem. Eddie, who always expected God to answer prayers, asked the couple "Were you surprised?"

Many couples from the mainland wanted to be married in Hawaii. Some asked Eddie to conduct the ceremonies in Lihue. Walter and Maryllis Hensel came from Wisconsin for their wedding. Plans and a small amount of counseling were done by phone ahead of time. The Hensels included Eddie in their wedding photo and later recounted his "enthusiasm, dedication, humor, Christian witness and counsel."

A nationally known football star had Eddie perform his marriage ceremony. The best man was another football player, Ed "Too Tall" Jones. During the service, Too Tall Jones kneeled so that he wouldn't rise so high over the little minister. Even on his knees, however, the football player may have been taller than Eddie.

One Valentine's Day, the newspaper reported that Eddie conducted 12 weddings. Who knows how many he performed each year. Some of the weddings were held in the Coco Palms Chapel, some in the Fern Grotto, others at the Lutheran church. Then there were helicopter weddings. A couple wanted to be married on a scenic bluff overlooking the ocean. The only way to get there was by helicopter. After checking out the spectacular vista with a preview trip, Eddie agreed and performed their wedding.

Eddie always used the Common Marriage Service. In some things Eddie was innovative, but when it came to the wedding ceremony and the sacraments he was traditional. He revered the Word of God and held great esteem for worship, although at times he abbreviated the liturgy.

The Destruction by Hurricane Iwa

Life at Lihue was like paradise in many ways for Eddie and the church until Hurricane Iwa hit.

As the storm approached, radio bulletins warned people to stay off the roads. On his way home from the Coco Palms Resort, Eddie could feel the gusting winds and see the waves crashing against the beach. Marie was worried until Eddie was safely home.

That night the wind roared. Around the island trees crashed to the ground, blocking many roads and bringing down power lines. People wondered if the fury would ever stop. With electricity out, people had to use candles. Waves slammed into the resorts and homes along the coast, causing extensive damage. At the parsonage, a falling tree branch broke a window.

Late that night a tremendous gust of wind hit the hilltop. Eddie and Marie heard a mighty crash. Grabbing his robe and a flashlight, Eddie headed out into the driving rain to see what had happened. The church was gone! All Eddie saw was a tumbled mass of timbers. Eddie murmured a prayer: "Lord, just give me strength to get it back up again."

Dawn revealed the full extent of the damage. When the wind ripped off the roof, the walls and tower had crumbled to the ground. Sections of the roof lay upside down in the cemetery. The tower had smashed into pieces when it hit the ground. The church had been literally lifted off its foundation.

Solace After the Storm

Eddie surveyed the damage to determine if there was any salvageable lumber. He carefully crawled under the timbers to see how badly the altar and chancel area had been damaged.

Church and altar guild member Gussie Schumacher walked over to check out the damage as well. She, too, crawled under the timbers to see if the communion ware could be salvaged. When she heard noise, she knew she wasn't alone. Figuring that it had to be Eddie, she shouted out, "Now there will be no looting, please!" Recognizing Gussie's voice, Eddie laughed. When they crawled back outside, they were joined by other church members. Everyone agreed that the church had to be rebuilt.

While they were talking, a television news crew came by and videotaped Eddie beside the damaged church. The reporter said, "Pastor Spirer, all of us

Hurricane Iwa

Dawn revealed the full extent of the damage to the Lihue Lutheran Church. When the wind ripped off the roof, the walls and tower had crumbled to the ground. Sections of the roof lay upside down in the cemetery. The tower had smashed into pieces when it hit the ground. The church had been literally lifted off its foundation.

After 11 months and with the help of $300,000 in donations, the church was rebuilt in 1983, with Eddie's supervision. Its cemetery (opposite page) is the final resting place of Eddie Spirer.

are sorry you lost your historic church."

Eddie quickly replied, "Oh no, we didn't lose the church! The church is the people and the church is fine! We just lost the building, and we will rebuild that stronger than before!" That night thousands on the islands saw Eddie on television as he stood by the ruins of the historic church.

After the big storm, the Hawaiian Council of Churches asked Eddie to write a Lenten devotion for distribution around the island. The meditation reads as follows:

Let not your heart be troubled. You believe in God, believe also in Me (John 14:1).

Iwa was all afternoon showing her ugliness. Blowing up a storm that tried our faith and surely separated the men from the boys. It was Marie's and my first experience of this nature. At first we thought it was fun to be in the comfort of the parsonage with windows rattling, while we watched trees swaying and shrubs bowing. But soon, with the loss of power and the absence of the radio report, it was easy for anxiety to creep in. The wind has a way of adding to the normal fear of the heart.

The fact that both of us were looking for a spot of safety indicated that we had need of assurance and comfort. We found that so fully in the oft repeated and familiar statement of Jesus, "Let not your heart be troubled. You believe in God, believe also in me."

How often we are troubled and full of fear because we look elsewhere. As soon as we fully yielded and allowed our faith to take control, we found ourselves in capable hands and heard Him ask, "You believe in God, trust me." Let the wind blow. The fury no longer annoyed us. We were in good hands.

Are you in good hands? He wants us to bring our fears and burdens and cast them all upon Him, for He cares for us.

So we trusted the Lord, and at once we were filled with a song of praise, although our hundred-year-old jewel of a church building was at our feet. The next morning the total loss came to its eighty-seven-year-old "Little Minister" as a challenge to rebuild and bring back another century of witness to the Church of All Nations nestled on a peaceful hill in Kauai.

"Let not your heart be troubled, just believe in God and trust Jesus."

For years Eddie had been sending an annual Christmas letter to visitors who had signed the church guest book. Many had been impressed with the colorful church and with its little minister. Most of them had heard through the media about the devastation of Hurricane Iwa and the damage to Eddie's church at Lihue.

Eddie Builds Again

Eddie wrote to these people telling them exactly what had happened to the Lihue church. He told them that he was praying and preparing to rebuild. Eddie asked them to pray with him, but he did not ask for money. He knew that the damage would be covered by the insurance.

The response to the letter was amazing. Each day a bundle of letters came addressed to "The Little Minister." Many friends sent assurances of their prayers and most added a generous check to help rebuild. The gifts totaled $300,000! Eddie was pleased, but not surprised. "I never ask for money," said Eddie. "I pray to the Lord and ask for His help and God has never failed me."

Lihue church members discussed what to do with the money since they were fully covered by insurance. They decided to use the $300,000 to rebuild the church and to deposit the insurance money for future ministry of the church.

Even with the funds available, rebuilding was a huge undertaking. Eddie led the project. It was completed in 11 months. All the bills were paid, and there was money in the bank. The dedication day was a wonderful celebration of thanksgiving and joy. Indeed, the church—both the people and the building—was stronger than before.

People all over the world heard about the church because of the hurricane. As a result, a stream of visitors, mostly tourists, attended services. This kept Eddie busy with ministry and making jelly rolls. At eighty-eight, Eddie had served 19 years longer than most ministers who generally retire at age sixty-five. He had been ill and had undergone surgery. It was time for him to be relieved of his pastoral burdens.

Aloha for Eddie

The aloha for the Little Minister was not an easy one. He had served faithfully and he had touched many lives. The congregation honored Eddie with a special luncheon.

The people of the island of Kauai also wanted to thank Eddie. To do this they gave him an unusual honor. Mayor Tony Kunimura proclaimed November 10, 1984, "Dr. Edward Spirer Day."

Eddie in Retirement

When Eddie retired from the Lihue congregation, he and Marie returned to California and purchased a home in Leisure World, between Los Angeles and San Diego. They lived there for a number of years until Eddie had a fall.

Retiring after 60 years of full-time ministry, Eddie is honored by the Lihue congregation, including Gussie Schaumacher (left) and Catherine Lo. The people of Kauai also joined in the celebration after Mayor Tony Kunimura declared November 10, 1984 as Dr. Eddie Spirer Day.

After that he suffered from dizzy spells. California Lutheran Homes had a care center nearby in Carlsbad-by-the-Sea. Eddie went there.

After he received a pacemaker, Eddie's condition improved and his blood pressure returned to normal. At the time, Eddie made it clear that if he became seriously ill, no heroic efforts were to be taken. He had lived a full life.

Many years had passed since that night Eddie had prayed for healing and made his covenant with God. God had healed him and Eddie had served his Lord faithfully.

"God heard my prayer and healed me. Imagine! I never had any trouble all these years with that sickness," Eddie said while in Carlsbad. "God is good and I am grateful!"

Eddie enjoyed his years at Carlsbad-by-the-Sea. The ministry he had blessed so much through the years was now blessing him. Carlsbad was part of the Lutheran Homes project that had begun with the Alhambra home and now consisted of eight homes. The ministry Eddie had helped start 43 years earlier was now a blessing to him. Yet Eddie was still giving. He often led chapel services in Carlsbad.

Eddie's Last Sermon

Sometimes Eddie spent the weekend at home with Marie. A few times they went back to worship at Hollywood Lutheran Church. One Saturday Eddie phoned Pastor Harry Durkee to tell him they were coming up the next day for Sunday services and he would like to preach. Harry said that would be fine.

54

But early Sunday morning, Eddie was quite sick. Marie called to tell Harry that they probably wouldn't be able to make the trip. But Eddie surprised Marie and insisted that they go. At Hollywood Lutheran, Harry Durkee offered Eddie a special pew and suggested he rest. "Not on your life," Eddie said. "I didn't come here to sit. I came to preach!"

And preach he did. It was a typical Spirer sermon, evangelical and warm. In closing, he asked everyone to join him in singing his favorite hymn, "Into my heart, into my heart, come into my heart, Lord Jesus. Come in today, come in to stay, come into my heart, Lord Jesus."

That day in Hollywood Lutheran Church, where he had been ordained sixty years earlier, Eddie preached his last sermon.

With the Lord Forever

In November 1990 Eddie suffered a massive stroke and never regained consciousness. While Eddie was in a coma, Pastor Quentin Garman came to the hospital to visit. As he held Eddie's hand, he prayed, "Lord, now let thy servant depart in peace."

That same day two unusual incidents took place. Pastor Harry Durkee and his wife, Norma, heard Eddie was failing and immediately drove down from Hollywood. Seeing how weak Eddie was, Pastor Durkee bent over and spoke into Eddie's ear, "Eddie, this is Harry and Norma. We wanted to come and be with you." Eddie immediately raised his head, seeming to know that they were there. They stayed for a while, then Pastor Durkee offered a prayer before leaving for home.

Later that evening Marie was sitting by Eddie's bed, holding his hand. Eddie had not spoken a word since the stroke. He seemed to be getting weaker and his breathing was slower. Suddenly Eddie raised his arm and pointed upward. He held that position for a moment, then his arm dropped. Moments later he stopped breathing.

When Harry Durkee heard how his dear friend had passed on, he asked, "Isn't that just like Eddie to choreograph even his last moment?" What did the gesture mean? Did Eddie know God was calling him home?

When Pastor Garman heard the news, he said, "Let the celebration begin. Eddie is with the Lord forever."

Eddie's funeral was where he had requested, in Hollywood Lutheran Church. He had said that if he didn't have it there, his friends would not believe that he was really dead. He was buried in Lihue, Hawaii, near the church that he had restored and later rebuilt. The plaque that marks his grave is inscribed:

A converted Jew, he served the Lord for 61 years. He leaves memorial of brick and stone in the 53 churches he built during the ten years he

The Rev. Doctor Edward N. Spirer, shown here New Year's Eve, 1988, died December 6, 1990. He was buried in Lihue, Hawaii, near the church that he had restored and later rebuilt.

served as Director of Church Extension for the Pacific Southwest Lutheran Synod. While pastor of Lihue Lutheran Church he restored the building in 1981 to celebrate its 100th anniversary, only to repeat the restoration when Hurricane Iwa leveled the church in November 1982. His Bagel and Jelly Roll Ministry, shared with a twinkle in his eye and a smile on his lips, brought joy and love to all he touched. He lived his faith and his testimony for his Savior was implanted in the heart of countless thousands for all eternity. His prayer for us: "Our Lord Jesus, you have endured the doubts and foolish questions of every generation. Forgive us for trying to be judge over you, and grant us the confident faith to acknowledge you as Lord. Amen."

APPENDIXES

APPENDIX A

What others said about Eddie Spirer at the time of his "retirement"

"'Behold, I am laying in Zion for a foundation a stone, a tested stone.' The Lord has been using you [Eddie] in a very real way to lay foundations for Him. The foundation stone has been and is the very precious tested stone, Christ Jesus our Lord. Some may think of what you have done in terms of building earthly buildings, but your ministry will always be thought of by me as one sent to lay this precious cornerstone in Zion. Upon this Precious Cornerstone, the Church will be built. Storms will come, but the structure of His Church will remain. May I add just a personal note for the many days we served together, and that simple note is just one of gratitude: 'Thank you Eddie.'"
—Dr. James P. Beasom Jr., President of the Synod

"Before the Seminary opened you designed and built offices for our faculty, a needed classroom, and prepared our chapel furnishings,—(sic) and paid for it yourself! You have blessed many a worthy enterprise in a rich and imaginative way, and have saved thousands of Kingdom dollars for the Cause. I am grateful to you for your helpfulness and friendship in a very personal way."
—Charles B. Foelsch, president, Pacific Lutheran Seminary

"All of us remember the months back in 1948-49 when you built our new church. What remains bright and clear in all our memories is the shining spirit of devotion you brought to this work, and the patient, persistent way in which you saw it through to completion, because it was 'the Lord's Work.' The treasured legacy of devotion has made a place for you in our hearts which no one else can ever take."
—Charles Smith, pastor, St. Luke's, Huntington Beach

"I feel your role in the developing of the Home for the Aged and the Camp proved to be a turning point in both instances. We were enabled to move out of the realm of wishful thinking into action. This I know has been multiplied in dozens of congregations where you have provided them facility for study and worship."
—John Stump, pastor, La Canada

"Beyond a doubt there is more of Dr. and Mrs. Spirer in the California Lutheran Home than in any other portion of the Church. From the very beginning of the Home, you have given of yourself without reserve in the preparation of the Home, the building of the cottages and the building of the new wing. Therefore we salute you and thank you and pray for you and Mrs. Spirer the choice blessings of our Lord."
—John Steinhaus, pastor, California Lutheran Home

"We deeply appreciate how you kept the costs down to a reasonable figure so that the construction of our camp could be a possibility. God has blessed our Church here on the West Coast through your skill, enterprise, and devotion. Not many of us can point too many concrete evidences of our labor. And I know you will never cease to be in construction. For if it isn't in stone,

wood, plaster and glass, it will be love and understanding in hearts and lives. For you are a BUILDER, either temples or bridges, and both are vital to the kingdom of God."
—Jack Foerster, director, Camp Yolijwa

"We are thankful for your zeal, your devotion and your stamina in carrying forth a difficult building program for our congregation. Nothing that we can say can express our gratitude in a sufficient way. Here in the Islands are two symbols of your handiwork."
—St. Paul's and the Lutheran Church of Honolulu.

We want to extend a sincere 'Mahalo Nui' for the many back-breaking hours you put in at these churches giving so generously of your time and talent until the cornerstone was carefully sealed in its resting place."
—Ernest Vetter, pastor, St. Paul's Lutheran Church, Honolulu

"Words cannot express our appreciation for what you did for us in our building program. Your spirit hovers in every corner and your name is mentioned often as we enjoy this wonderful building. Personally may I add you shall always have a warm spot in my heart, for I value your friendship a great deal and I know of no one whom I like better."
—F. W. Heinecken, pastor, Trinity Lutheran Church, Riverside

"Please accept by deepest thanks for your untiring efforts and hard labor in erecting our Church. It would not have been possible without your wonderful cooperation. Your unselfish help enabled me to express my thanks for the permission to come to the USA by erecting a church to the glory of God. This will never be forgotten."
—Bruno Ederma, pastor, Norco

"Most of our people remember you with affection as the 'good Pastor Eddie.' Your high good humor in no little measure helped sustain the morale of a little congregation which for a time was without pastor when you were leading the building program. At our tenth anniversary you graciously brought a message of faith and raised a certain nostalgia for the helter-skelter days of the early building programs. Be assured that our prayers go with you to the quieter waters of retirement with full appreciation for what you have done."
—Vlad Blenko, pastor, St. Peter's by the Sea, San Diego

"We here at Trinity are grateful for you constructed two units for us in our building program. We have witnessed in you one of the hardest working Christians that we have ever been associated with. You are a man that not only has a talent in the building trades, but a Christian that is not afraid to witness for His Lord no matter where or what he might be doing."
—William Bowman, pastor, Trinity Lutheran Church, Pomona

"The tallest spire that we shall remember and be forever grateful for is not the one you formed of mortar and stone but of faith in our Lord Jesus Christ. 'Tis of God's building, that one so short can stand so tall in the sight of God and man."
—Lloyd Sturtevant, pastor, Faith Lutheran Church, Long Beach

APPENDIX B

Letter sent to friends by Eddie Spirer after Hurricane Iwa struck in November 1982.

Dearly Beloved:

It is with a heavy heart that I pen these lines, yet a big hope fills me with encouragement. Our God is able, able to use all this to the glory of His Son.

What a privilege we have as Christians to show our color and prove our faith that "all things work together for good to them that love the Lord."

No doubt you are fully acquainted with our loss. T.V. coverage brought phone calls of sincere concern. Thank God not one hair of my spare head is out of place. Marie, too, proved to be a real trouper and in her ability and skill is a tremendous help to both me and the Congregation. It could well be that the Lord has reserved this day of need for our ministry. We just pray (and hope you will join us) for physical strength to carry on in His Name.

We are not one bit concerned. We know in whom we believe and He is able. We do believe that you desire a share in the rugged task of digging ourselves out and to bring back the glory of former days to the "Little Church on German Hill."

Our plan definitely is to honor those who labored so faithfully to establish the witness of Christ on stricken Kauai by restoring the Church to its original state.

My brother Irv, whose profession is architecture and for years has been an outstanding one, has offered his service without charge to make the plans possible. With the aid of photographs, we should be able to accomplish this. With our present-day methods of construction, a repeat (God forbid) of a similar disaster should leave us intact.

At any rate, we sorrow not for the loss of building—thank God we still have a Church. I assure you the body of believers are still intact and full of hope.

God bless you for your prayers in the past as well as your interest. Just remember us now and uphold our hands in prayer and support. We have always been grateful for your past feelings in Christ for us.

Our Newsletter was all ready for mailing when the storm arrived. For some unknown reason, I neglected to take them to the Post Office; hence this letter to let you know God is answering your prayer and we are here to do His will and maintain His testimony.

We love you much,
Sincerely,
The Little Minister & Marie

APPENDIX C

A chronology of the life of Edward Nathaniel Spirer

1895	Born on January 23 in Wilmington, Delaware to Frank and Dena Markowitz Spirer.
1906	Bar Mitzvah
1913	Graduated from Wilmington High School, Wilmington, Delaware
1913-1915	Attended University of Delaware
1916-1918	Attended University of Pennsylvania
1918-1921	Works in the construction business with his father
1918	Meets Wilhemena Dettling
1918	Attends Zion Lutheran Church and is given his first Bible
1921	Frank Spirer orders his son to leave home
1921	Eddie moves to Los Angeles
1921	Eddie is baptized in First Lutheran Church, Los Angeles
1921-1922	Eddie works as a carpenter in Los Angeles
1923	Eddie joins Hollywood Lutheran Church
1923	Eddie and Mena get married
1923	Eddie gets his contractor's license
1926-1929	Eddie ill with nephritis
1929-1930	Eddie attends Western Seminary in Nebraska
1930	Eddie is ordained as a minister
1930	Eddie is installed at St. Luke's in Omaha, Nebraska
1931	Eddie and Mena return to Los Angeles
1931	St. Matthew's Lutheran Church organized in North Hollywood. Eddie is the pastor
1934	Eddie is given the nickname "The Little Minister"
1935	New building dedicated at St. Matthew's
1942-1945	Eddie serves as a U.S. Army Chaplain
1946	The Alhambra Home property is renovated
1947	Alhambra Home property dedicated
1948-1958	Eddie works as director of Church Extension
1958	Eddie honored at Lutheran convention as his church extension work is completed
1958-1976	Eddie is a supply minister
1973-1976	Eddie is pastor of St. Michael Lutheran Church in Sun Valley
1974	Mena Dettling Spirer dies on January 22
1976	Installed as pastor of Lihue Lutheran Church in Hawaii
1976-1981	Lihue Church renovated
1981	Lihue Church dedicated and Eddie marries Marie Carranza
1982	Hurricane Iwa destroys Lihue church
1983	Reconstructed Lihue church dedicated on November 13
1984	Dr. Edward Spirer Day on the Island of Kauai (November 10)
1984	Eddie retires, moves with Marie to Laguna Hills, California
1990	On December 6, Eddie dies in Carlsbad, California

APPENDIX D

Excerpts from meditations at Eddie Spirer's funeral, December 15, 1990.

"Grace to you from God the Father and from our Lord Jesus Christ. We are here today to recognize the ministry of Eddie Spirer who has been a powerful witness in our lives and in the life of this Church.

"Eddie Spirer as a 'builder of church buildings.' Beautiful buildings that served well as marvelous first units. Many of them are still serving congregations.

"But Eddie was also a 'builder of community,' the community of God's people. Wherever he went his witness, his love for life, his love for the Lord exuded from the community. People loved to be a part of the community where Eddie was Pastor. Many of you have eaten jelly rolls that he made. He had an ability to build community, and we thank God for his gifts.

"I am also thankful today that 'Eddie was a confessor.' He was one who came to love the Lord and he was one who was unashamed to proclaim that Jesus Christ is Lord. He came to know how important it was in his life that God through Jesus Christ had loved him and accepted him. One of the things that was so important in my life was to hear Eddie say what the Lord Jesus meant to him. And to say to the rest of us in the Church that the great love of God is too good to keep and we ought to be willing to get out there and tell the world how much God loves them and how good Jesus Christ is!" —Bishop J. Roger Anderson

"When I visited our Church in Lihue in the summer of 1988, visiting with the members and friends of that congregation, I began to hear the multitude of stories about Eddie Spirer. I was blessed by that and glad to know that Eddie Spirer was part of the Church to which I had been called to serve.

"Today I am reminded that the Body of Christ is bigger than we ever imagined. God has blessed His Church with a multitude of persons and gifts. While I did not get to know him as many of you did, I am an inheritor of that legacy that God gave us through him. I am blessed by it. And so as his Bishop in these last years of his life it is my privilege to say to you this morning on behalf of the Evangelical Lutheran Church in America, the Pacifica Synod, 'Thanks be to God for the life and ministry of Pastor Eddie Spirer.'"
—Bishop Robert Miller

"From the Gospel, the first chapter, Luke quotes a young woman singing praise to God: 'Oh, magnify the Lord, O my soul.' It seems to me that represents Eddie Spirer all the way. 'My soul doth magnify the Lord.' To magnify is to make something bigger. It is not a microscope but a 'magnificat.' Eddie knew from his Mosaic background that somehow God was great. He knew and we know that God has a way of doing things that are far beyond what we want to do. Never put a limit on what God can do!

"You see, for Eddie God was One who revealed Himself in many different ways. He had a great God. A God who was revealing Himself. Part of the truth that we have known in the years we have known Eddie Spirer and to which we aspire, if you will. And we have come today to praise this great God, as Eddie praised Him.

"Always lifting up people, instead of putting them down. Instead of lowering them to his size, he was constantly raising them to the stature of God. He was magnifying God. The holiness of God. The love of God. The hope that God gives. You can't read through that Magnificat without being impressed withe the knowledge of the history of Israel and how it was being fulfilled in this Christ.

"Eddie knew the Old Testament, too, and he knew a God who is eternal in dimension. And we give thanks to God for what we have learned from him. Eddie, like the Wise Men, came from the East. They saw a star and followed it. They brought gold, frankincense and myrrh. Eddie came from the East. Saw a star, brought hammer, nails and a saw. All of it to glorify God. It seems to me that we have learned some things from Eddie here. That we've got to do business with what we've got! Eddie wasn't a candidate for the Lakers. He was almost too short for this pulpit. But the thing is, he had something to give, and he gave it first. And he expected other people to give it. Think of those places of worship that Eddie has built. Because he with his inimitable life, could not only design but construct and then preach in those same buildings.

"Eddie was a guy who could get other people to do things. It's a strange thing, how he could tell people what he needed to build all of those churches, and they would respond! You know, Eddie had a way of making people feel that they were really doing something. In a way, he was God moving people to do God's work. There is a place in the Kingdom for people like this.

"He made a lot of people miserable. You know that. He wasn't the easiest guy in the world to live with. Bishops don't know about that, but people do. But we're grateful for him.

"Today we thank Hollywood Lutheran Church, whose members sheltered Eddie when he was so sick many years before he went into the ministry. And so then as we return him to God we say, God bless him and God bless us, and keep us forever singing, 'O magnify the Lord for He is good. His mercy endureth forever.'"
—Bishop Lloyd Burke

APPENDIX E

Eddie Spirer's Spires—The Churches Eddie Built

Church/Project Name	Location	Type of Unit
1935		
St. Matthew's	North Hollywood, CA	Church
1943		
Lockheed	North Hollywood, CA	Chapel
Alhambra Home	Alhambra, CA	Renovated Home for the Aged
Salem Lutheran	Whittier, CA	Church
1948-1949		
St. Paul's Lutheran	Vallejo. CA	Church
St. Andrew Lutheran	San Mateo, CA	Church
Beverly Hills Lutheran	Beverly Hills, CA	Expansion
Trinity Lutheran	Pomona, CA	First Unit
Good Shepherd Lutheran	Altadena, CA	Church
Christ Lutheran	Pacific Beach, CA	First Unit
St. Peter's-by-the-Sea	San Diego, CA	Church
Luther Memorial Lutheran	Burbank, CA	Church
Lakewood Village Lutheran	Long Beach, CA	Church
St. Luke's Lutheran	Huntington Beach, CA	Church
Gloria Dei	Long Beach, CA	Chapel
St. Paul's Lutheran	Monterey Park, CA	First Unit
Our Savior's Lutheran	Orange, CA	First Unit
1950		
Inglewood Lutheran	Inglewood, CA	Sunday School
St. Luke's Lutheran	Long Beach, CA	Church
Our Savior's Lutheran	Alhambra, CA	Church
Beverly Hills Lutheran	Beverly Hills, CA	Fire Damage, Repair
1951		
Epiphany Lutheran	San Leandro, CA	Chapel
Christ Lutheran	San Diego, CA	Chapel and Education Unit
St. James Lutheran	Richmond, CA	Chapel
Trinity Lutheran	Alameda, CA	Church
Sunset Lutheran	San Francisco, CA	Church
Trinity Lutheran	Manhattan Beach, CA	Church
1952-1953		
Our Savior's Lutheran	Alhambra, CA	Church
Bethany Lutheran	San Jose, CA	Church
Transfiguration Lutheran	Los Angeles, CA	Church
Pacific Lutheran Seminary	Berkeley, CA	School

Church/Project Name	Location	Type of Unit
Trinity Lutheran	Pomona, CA	Church
Good Shepherd Lutheran	Reno, NV	Church
Grace Lutheran	Richmond, CA	Church and Education Unit
St. Paul's Lutheran	Globe, AZ	Church
St. John's Lutheran	Norwalk, CA	Church
Bethany Lutheran	Norco, CA	Church
Calif. Lutheran Homes	Alhambra, CA	Cottages
First Lutheran	San Bernardino, CA	Church
Honolulu Lutheran	Honolulu, HI	Church
United Lutheran	Santa Ana, CA	Church
Grace Lutheran	Culver City, CA	Church
1954-1955		
Calif. Lutheran Homes	Alhambra, CA	Infirmary
St. Peter's-by-the Sea	San Diego, CA	Church
St. Paul's Lutheran	Honolulu, HI	Chapel, Education Unit
St. Matthew's Lutheran	North Hollywood, CA	New Unit
First Lutheran	Glendale, CA	Church
St. Mark's Lutheran	San Fernando, CA	First Unit
Mt. of Olives Lutheran	Phoenix, AZ	First Unit
Faith Lutheran	Fresno, CA	Church
First United Lutheran	San Francisco, CA	Church
Calvary Lutheran	Azusa, CA	Church
St. Paul's Lutheran	Monterey Park, CA	Sanctuary
1956-1957		
Messiah Lutheran	Redwood City, CA	
Trinity Lutheran	Riverside, CA	Church
Redeemer Lutheran	El Monte, CA	Church
St. Andrew's Lutheran	Van Nuys, CA	Church
Calif. Lutheran Homes	Alhambra, CA	Expansion
Trinity Lutheran	Pomona, CA	Education Unit
St. Paul's Lutheran	Monterey Park, CA	Education Unit
Bethany Lutheran	Santa Clara, CA	First Unit
Camp Yolijwa	Yucaipa, CA	Camp
St. James Lutheran	Richmond, CA	Education Unit, Fellowship Hall
Bethany Lutheran	Norco, CA	Church
Salem Lutheran	Whittier, CA	Sanctuary
1983		
Lihue Lutheran Church	Lihue, HI	Restored

65

APPENDIX F

Bibliography and Resources

1. Oral History of Dr. Edward Spirer. Taken by Ross F. Hidy, December 2-3, 1987, at Carlsbad.

2. Oral Histories: Quentin Garman, Carlsbad, CA; Harry Mumm, Scotts Valley, CA; Christian Thearle, Salem, OR; Charles Smith, Medford, OR; Howard Logan, Los Angeles, CA; Harry Durkee, Burbank, CA; Roger Rogahn, Los Angeles, CA; Wayne Pfundstein, Burbank, CA; Kathryn Lee, Chicago, IL; Carl Tambert, Cupertino, CA; Catherine Lo, Lihue, HI; Gussie Schumacher, Lihue, HI; Arthur Hansen, Seattle, WA.

3. *Pacific Southwest Lutheran,* edited by Richard Bennett, 1954-1974.

4. California Synod yearbooks, ULCA.

5. United Lutheran Church (California Synod) archives.

6. Evangelical Lutheran Church in America archives, Chicago, IL: Correspondence of Dr. Franklin Clark Fry and Dr. Elwood Bowman.

7. *The Lutheran,* magazine.

8. *Beasom the Builder,* Lutheran Pioneer Press, Vol. 1, 1986 (LHCW).

9. *The Fruitage of Fifty Years, the Fiftieth Anniversary Book of the California Synod (1891-1941),* edited by Dr. John Edward Hoick.

10. The California Synod and Pacific Southwest Synod of the United Lutheran Church in America, Minutes; 1930-1976.

11. United Lutheran Church in America, Minutes; 1930-1958.

12. Lutheran School of Theology, archives, Chicago, IL.

13. Zion Lutheran Church, archives, Wilmington, DE.

14. St. Matthew's Lutheran Church, archives, North Hollywood, CA.

15. Grace Lutheran Church, archives, Richmond, CA.

16. Bond, Lutheran Brotherhood, Minneapolis, MN.

17. San Diego Convention, tributes to Eddie Spirer, 1958.

18. *Burbank Daily Review,* August 1, 1973, Burbank, CA.

19. *Garden Island,* Lihue, HI.

20. *Messiah Hebrew Lutheran,* p. 5, Jan. 1930.

21. Correspondence: Barbara Spirer Gilbert, Dr. John A. Monroe, Catherine Lo, Marian DeGennaro, John Stimmons, Morgan Edwards, John Stump, Quentin Garman, E. Dale Click, Robert Marshall, James R. Crumley Jr., Kenneth Senfit, Malcolm Minnick, J. Benner Weaver, Lawrence Baietti, Ray Stiffler, Renee Bonker Geiger, David Robison, Ray Anderson, A. G. Fjellman, J. Roger Anderson, Robert Miller, Lloyd Burke, Carl V. Tambert, Robert Inslee, Howard Lenhardt, Harry Mumm, Wayne Pfundstein, Mrs. John Foerster, Clarice and Tom Allport, Jean Frank, Bernice Dixon, Karl Kniseley II, Gerald Strickler, Ginny Wagener, David Peterson, Forest Lawn Memorial Park, Kay and Otis Lee, Christian Thearle, Robert Rogahn, Irv Moline, Harry Durkee, William Lesher, Walter Stuhr, Carl Moyer, Charles Smith, John Steinhaus, Philip Jordan, University of Pennsylvania School of Architecture.

22. Photographs were acquired from: The personal papers of Dr. Edward and Marie Spirer; Barbara Spirer Gilbert; Catherine Lo; Dr. John A. Monroe; Robert Inslee; various Lutheran churches; regional archives at Pacific Lutheran Seminary, Berkeley, CA; *Lutheran* magazine archives, Chicago, IL; Zion Lutheran Church, Wilmington, DE; *Pacific Southwest Lutheran,* Richard Bennett, editor; Raymond Anderson.

These research materials have been deposited in the Regional Archives at Pacific Lutheran Theological Seminary, Berkeley, California as "The Edward Spirer Papers."

For more information about Jewish evangelism contact:

Jews for Jesus
60 Haight Street
San Francisco, CA 94102-5895

415-864-2600
Email: jfj@jews-for-jesus.org;
WWW:http://www.jews-for-jesus.org

For more information about Lutheran history contact:

Dr. Ross Hidy
The Lutheran History Center of the West
5242 Park Highlands Blvd.
Concord, CA 94521-3706

If you enjoyed the testimony of Eddie Spirer, you will want to read the exciting testimonies of other Jewish believers. Also available from Purple Pomegranate Productions:

Testimonies edited by Ruth Rosen is a compilation of stories about Jewish believers from various walks of life. A lawyer, a cop, a heart transplant recipient, a peace activist, a successful business man and others tell of how Y'shua changed their lives. The 320-page book sells for $5.95 (BK046) (Purple Pomegranate Productions).

Disowned by Steve Cohen recounts the exciting way in which as aspiring young Jewish lawyer became a Christian missionary instead. When Steve accepted Christ, like Eddie Spirer, he was disowned by his family. But there is a surprising twist as Steve is reconciled with his seriously ill father. This testimony will inspire all Christians and will encourage those who are praying for unbelieving family members. This booklet sells for $1.95 (BK063) (Purple Pomegranate Productions).

Betrayed by Stan Telchin is the story of a Jewish businessman whose life was turned upside down when his daughter challenged him to consider Y'shua as Messiah. In a wholehearted effort to disprove her faith, he finds the Messiah. This 140-page book sells for $7.95 (BK021) (Baker Books).

To order any of the above books, please write to Purple Pomegranate Productions, 80 Page Street, San Francisco, CA 94102-5914 or call 415-864-3900.

Please add 10 percent for shipping on all orders. California residents must add $7\frac{1}{4}$ percent sales tax.